Collins
LITTLE BOOKS

C000108486

CRAFT
BEER

HarperCollins Publishers
Westerhill Road
Bishopbriggs
Glasgow
G64 2QT

First Edition 2018

10 9 8 7 6 5 4 3 2

© HarperCollins Publishers 2018

ISBN 978-0-00-827120-6

Collins® is a registered trademark
of HarperCollins Publishers Limited

www.collins.co.uk

A catalogue record for this book is
available from the British Library

Author: Dominic Roskrow

Typeset by
Davidson Publishing Solutions

Printed and bound in China by
RR Donnelley APS Co Ltd

Contents

About the Author

Dominic Roskrow is an award-winning drinks writer and magazine editor. He specialises in whisky and has written 12 books on the subject. He has edited *The Spirits Business*, *Club Mirror*, *Pub Business*, and *Whisky Magazine*, writes a spirits column for *Drinks International*, and has contributed to dozens of newspapers and magazines across the world. He was Fortnum & Mason Drinks Writer of the Year in 2015. His most recent book, *Whisky: Japan*, was chosen as Britain's best spirits book in the Gourmand Food and Drink Awards and is shortlisted for the title of Gourmand World's Best Spirit Book.

Dominic is one of only a few people to be chosen as a Keeper of the Quaich for his work on Scotch whisky, and to be appointed a Kentucky Colonel for his promotion of bourbon. Dominic is an avid Leicester City and All Blacks fan, and loves loud heavy rock music.

Talking about a revolution

Take a look at today's craft brewing industry and it's hard to believe that as recently as the turn of the millennium the perception of beer brewing was of scruffy, hippy types in sandals, geekily discussing secondary fermentations.

Back then it was all about real ale in the United Kingdom, and about proper beer in America. To outsiders the battle for beer was just that – a campaign against mass produced and homogenous beer, and especially lager. Unless it was a lager produced in Continental Europe. Or in a garage in Portland, Oregon.

The problem was that some of the alternatives weren't particularly appealing. Flat, scuzzy, cloudy concoctions might have been considered real by the diehards, but for many of the rest of us, they were just really bad.

Around that time, though, something changed. And when it did, it changed fast.

As Editor of *Beers of the World*, I remember sitting one Saturday evening sipping a new American craft beer – something from Rogue if I remember correctly – waiting to be interviewed on an American radio programme about beer. I could hear the two hosts on the show chatting about some new ale or other, and I recall being amazed by their passion and enthusiasm, and their knowledge of their subject. It was unnerving.

And that sort of passion flowed through the United States from Alaska to the Alamo as craft brewing took hold, as scores of enthusiasts turned their home brewing hobby into a business. Some brewers set out modestly and chose to stay that way.

Some started small but evolved into substantial businesses, moving to ever more sizeable premises and creating new jobs as they went. Some had grandiose aspirations from the outset, and are now living their dream.

Perhaps inevitably the United Kingdom would follow. All the pieces were in place due to years of work by the Campaign for Real Ale and organisations such as the Small Independent Brewers' Association (SIBA), which has now morphed into the Society of Independent Brewers, and the Independent Family Brewers of Britain (IFBB). Regional brewers were becoming more adventurous as they sought to create a niche for their beers among the plethora of brands marketed by big producers. Outstanding beer writers and a new generation of bloggers were writing about craft beer to a curious and broadminded beer community. Home brewing has long been popular in Britain, and some home brewers had become very good at it. Beer tourism to Belgium, The Netherlands and France had grown in popularity, and regional and small brewers were thriving due to favourable tax breaks.

When the phenomenon swept through Britain, the new producers carried with them many traditional European breweries with histories going back centuries, paying tribute to them, trying to reproduce their specific styles of beer, and resurrecting old redundant recipes.

Today's craft brewers come in all shapes and sizes. Of course the usual suspects are in the mix, and there are countless stories of beer-loving friends turning long-held dreams of making exciting beers into reality. But there are less obvious candidates, too:

solicitors and accountants who have turned their backs on the hustle and bustle of city life to embrace something altogether more sedate and satisfying; farmers who have turned a spare outbuilding into a brewery; restaurateurs and pub licensees keen to offer customers a home produced beer.

But while the supply of new beers was dramatic and impressive, what turned microbrewing into a phenomenon was the seemingly endless supply of keen consumers who were ready and willing to explore tastes and styles. Well travelled and familiar with exotic food and drink abroad, a new generation of drinkers was turning its back on homogenous and globalised products and was starting to seek out drinks with heritage, history and provenance.

There are other factors, too. The new drinkers are a health-conscious bunch, and prefer quality over quantity. But conversely, that also means that they're more open to sipping one or two pints of stronger alcohol, or drinking smaller 33cl or 25cl measures from a bottle of beer with a high alcohol content, rather than traditional session pints from the tap. Many of them are keen to seek out something new and exciting rather than drink what their parents drank. Many understand that there are craft beer styles that have little in common with traditional bitter or lager, and they not only don't care, they positively welcome the challenge such beers offer them. Many are eager to learn about them and explore further.

All of this was fuelled by the arrival of the Internet. It allowed small businesses to compete with large ones without the need for big advertising budgets, and to find a ready audience for their creative ideas. Enthusiasts are able to use social media and online blogs to draw attention to their discoveries. The Internet has become an educational tool, helping beer lovers understand more about even the most obscure porters, pale ales or sour beers.

Microbrewing has changed the face of our pubs and bars. The colourful chalkboard, with its zany names, varying ABVs, and brief taste descriptors, has become an increasingly visible road map for scores of patrons who see every trip into a licensed premises as a personal adventure and a journey of discovery. Leading supermarkets have shelves stacked with attractive bottles and, increasingly, cans. Upmarket supermarket chain Waitrose now sells single bottles of craft lagers that cost more than a bottle of wine.

They say what goes up must come down, and there are plenty of people who have predicted that the craft industry can't defy gravity indefinitely, and that an overcrowded marketplace will inevitably mean that some brewers will crash and burn.

By 2018 there were signs that in America at least, the number of new brewers was peaking, and some are starting to fall away. Inevitably, beer drinkers will separate the wheat from the chaff, and poorer products will not survive. But our palates have been changed forever; we have higher expectations of what beer can and should be, and the days of lifetime loyalty to one or two brands are long gone. If you have any doubts that craft brewing is a fad that will fade and die, then take a long, hard look at what even the most tame outlets are now offering, and at the way the global giants are trying to jump on the microbrewing bandwagon.

Never has it been a more exciting time for beer drinkers.

Cheers – don't mind if I do.

What is craft beer?

In late 2017 American organisation the Brewers Association (BA), publishers of craftbeer.com, launched a campaign to crowdfund the purchase of Anheuser-Busch, the makers of Budweiser.

The BA needs to raise a highly improbable – bordering on impossible – $213 billion, and while the campaign, called Take Craft Back, has its tongue firmly in its cheek, the underlying message is a very serious one: craft beer is under threat from global corporations intent on tapping into the large pool of beer drinkers, while stepping on anyone who gets in their way.

By the end of 2017 Anheuser-Busch had bought six craft brewers and was making inroads into major distribution channels. Other international drinks companies have also acquired craft breweries. Their beers are presented as if they are still made in a small farm shed in Michigan, but they are a con. Often they taste nothing like the original version – and this is not a good thing.

So what exactly constitutes a craft or microbrewer? This is not an easy question to answer.

The standard dictionary definition of craft is 'a skill, particularly in a trade'. This definition works for craft brewing, but it begs the question: isn't all beermaking a craft under this definition?

Wikipedia defines a microbrewery or craft brewery as 'one that produces small amounts of beer, typically much smaller than large-scale corporate breweries, and is independently owned. Such breweries are generally characterised by their emphasis on quality, flavour and brewing technique.'

This definition is grossly inadequate and incomplete; the last part is based on subjective evaluation, and there can be no place for that in a watertight definition. And what constitutes small? An American brewer and a British brewer may have very different ideas of what the word means, and one person's shed may be another's mansion.

More importantly, if a brewery grows due to consumer demand, but continues to make beer the same way but just on a bigger scale, does it then cease to be a craft brewery? And at what size does this happen?

So size can't be at the core of our definition of what craft brewing is. And although the word 'craft' implies an aspect of quality, our definition can't be totally about quality either. Big doesn't necessarily mean bad, as fans of Marston's Pedigree or Guinness will attest. Conversely, it's highly unlikely that the retired New York stockbroker brewing his first golden ale will hit on the perfect beer at his first attempt. He will almost certainly not make anything nearly as good as the makers of Adnams, Speckled Hen and many other great beers, perfected by skilled craftsmen over generations.

Wikipedia also has a definition for a microdistillery, '… a small, often boutique-style, distillery established to produce beverage grade spirit alcohol in relatively small quantities.'

This is more helpful, because of the word 'boutique', which can be used to mean 'a business serving a sophisticated or specialised clientele'.

This is much better. The definition nods toward the concept of size but makes it an issue of demand as well as supply. The word 'business' implies a level of care and professionalism, and by using the words 'sophisticated and specialised clientele' some concept of quality is brought into the frame. Not only that, but there is a strong implication that if there was a surge in demand from that sophisticated and specialised clientele, the business would still be a boutique one, even if it correspondingly grew to serve the increased demand.

This works for a definition of craft or microbrewing, too. If someone produces a beer that becomes popular so that the business has to grow to meet demand then, under our definition, this remains a craft operation, providing no compromise is made on the quality of their product, and there is no sell-out of the producer's original aspirations or ideals.

Perhaps, then, a craft brewery can be defined as 'any brewery that starts out as an independent boutique operation with the intention of making a bespoke and individual beer, and which stays true to the ideals of creating premium and quality beers no matter what happens to it.'

Under this definition it does not matter whether you're brewing in a traditional way or attempting something innovative. Nor whether you're brewing by hand on ancient equipment or have a state-of-the-art microbrewery. And it doesn't matter what ingredients you decide to use as long as the purpose is to enhance and enrich your beer, and not to save money or cut corners.

Glance at many of the websites of the craft brewers featured in this book and they will have a statement about what they set out to achieve with their beers, or they describe how they came into being. In all cases they would fit the definition above. Anheuser-Busch clearly does not.

Beer styles

Alt: A German-style brown ale. Alt translates as 'old' in German, and traditionally Altbiers are conditioned for longer than normal.

Belgian ale: Ales under approximately 7.0% ABV that do not fit other categories. Colour ranges from golden to deep amber.

Belgian blonde: Typically fruity, moderately malty, sweet, quite spicy, easy-drinking, copper-coloured ale.

Belgian strong pale ale: Treat with caution, due to high alcohol content. Expect a complex and powerful ale, yet delicate with rounded flavours.

Berliner weisse: a top-fermented, bottle-conditioned wheat beer. The taste is refreshing, tart, sour and acidic, with a lemony-citric fruit sharpness.

Bière de garde: From Northern France. Golden to deep copper or light brown in colour and characterised by a toasted malt aroma, slight malt sweetness in flavour, and medium hop bitterness.

Bitter: A gold to copper colour, with a biscuity malt and hoppy flavour, and medium to high bitterness.

Brown ale: Colour ranges from reddish-brown to dark brown. Beers termed brown ale include sweet low-alcohol beers, medium strength amber beers of moderate bitterness and malty but hoppy beers.

Dubbel: A rich malty beer with some spicy phenolic nuttiness. Mild hop bitterness with no lingering hop flavours.

Dunkel: Traditionally from Bavaria. Smooth, full-bodied, rich and complex, but without being heady or heavy. They boast brilliant ruby hues from the large amount of Munich malts used.

Farmhouse ale: Another name for Saison beers.

Golden ale: Pale, well-hopped and quenching beer developed in the 1980s. Strengths range from 3.5% to 5.3%.

Gose: An unfiltered wheat beer made with 50–60% malted wheat, which creates a cloudy yellow colour and provides a refreshing crispness and a touch of brine.

Gueuze: A traditional Belgian blend of young and old lambics, which are then blended, bottled and aged for two to three years to produce a drier, fruitier and more intense style of lambic.

Hefeweisse: German style of wheat beer made with a typical ratio of 50:50, or even higher, wheat. Has flavours of banana and cloves with an often dry and tart edge, some spiciness, bubblegum or notes of apples.

Imperial stout: Imperial stouts are usually extremely dark brown to black in colour and are intensely malty, deeply roasted and sometimes with accents of dark fruit and chocolate. Imperial stouts are strong and generally exceed 8.0% ABV.

IPA – India Pale Ale: The darling of craft brewing. It is stronger and more bitter than standard pale ale – and was pioneered in England in the early 19th century. There are worldwide varieties. The American version is bigger and bolder with grapefruit, pine, and citrus flavours.

Kölsch – from Köln: Light, delicate top-fermented beer with a dry finish.

Lambic: Naturally fermented with wild yeasts. Dry, sour and acidic, it's very much a specialist taste, and has grapefruit-like fruitiness. Closer in character to cider or fino sherry.

Old ale: Dark and malty and often of a higher alcoholic strength.

Pale ale: Hoppy and malty flavour and a golden to amber colour. British pale ales can be quite bitter; American-style pale ales have more citrus notes.

Pilsener: Well-hopped, with spicy, herbal, or floral aroma and flavour, with some citrus-like zesty hoppy bitterness.

Pilsner: From Bohemia in the Czech Republic. Medium- to full-bodied. Characterised by high carbonation and tangy Czech varieties of hops that impart floral aromas and a crisp, bitter finish.

Porter: Traditional and historical English beer. Black or chocolate malt gives the porter its dark brown colour. Porters are often well hopped and so heavily malted. There is considerable diversity in style but porters may be sweet.

Saison: Distinctive Belgian-style beer with lactic character and fruity, goaty and / or leather-like aromas and flavours. Specialty ingredients (including spices) may contribute a unique and signature character.

Schwarzbier: Refreshing, dark lagered German beer.

Sour beer: Covers a number of styles but with an intentionally acidic, tart or sour taste. Examples include lambics, gueuze and Flanders red ale.

Stout: Dry, roast and butter.

Tripel: Bright yellow to gold in colour. Complex, spicy, fruity and estery, with a sweet finish. Tend to be high in alcohol.

Witbier: Light, fluffy body and tart, lemony finish. Textured with wheat, very yeasty, and with pungent spices and hints of herbs.

Wood aged beers: Beer matured in oak casks. The casks come from various sources.

3 Monts

PRODUCER: Brasserie de St-Sylvestre

AREA OF ORIGIN: Saint Sylvestre Cappel, France

VARIETY: Golden ale

ABV: 8.5%

WEBSITE: www.brasserie-st-sylvestre.com

Brasserie de St-Sylvestre takes the view that the future of small brewers requires looking backwards to traditional brewing methods. It believes the expense of modern mechanisation has favoured the big brewing companies, pointing out that of 2000 small village breweries at the beginning of the 20th century, only 30 remain open now, and two-thirds of those are in the Nord-Pas-de-Calais. In order to survive, it argues, these small breweries have specialised in traditional beers, in contrast to the big boys. 3 Monts is one such ale, a throwback to another era with big, fruity and hoppy flavours. This ale has a light grassy nose. On the palate it starts sweet and malty, with softly sour wine-like characters and a decent bitter mouthfeel. It has a bitter and dryish finish. A great and refreshing but strong and tasty golden ale.

Abominable Winter Ale

PRODUCER: Hopworks Urban Brewery

AREA OF ORIGIN: Portland, USA

VARIETY: American IPA

ABV: 7.3%

WEBSITE: www.hopworksbeer.com

Hopworks is a brewery in Portland Oregon that makes a wide range of beers, both as core offerings and as seasonal releases. Abominable Winter Ale is made with organic Northwest hops and organic malt, and the brewery describes it as a complex floral, spicy, and citrusy beer. Despite its weighty alcoholic content, it is surprisingly easy to drink, with a medium-full mouthfeel and a distinct and enjoyable hoppiness. The taste mixes citrus and resinous hops notes with some light sweetness. There is some limited bitterness, with good floral notes. The body is fuller than average and there's a nice mixture of malt and fresh hops notes.

Hopworks has now made its range of beers available in attractive and colourful cans as well as traditional bottles, and includes ciders in its portfolio.

Amarillo Sour

PRODUCER: Chorlton Brewing Company

AREA OF ORIGIN: Manchester, England

VARIETY: Sour beer

ABV: 5.4%

WEBSITE: www.chorltonbrewingcompany.com

Sour beer is beer that has an intentionally acidic, tart or sour taste. The most common sour beer styles are Belgian: lambics, gueuze and Flanders red ale. The sourness is created by natural yeasts that would have found their way into beers before the introduction of the sterilised conditions associated with modern breweries. Amarillo Sour is based on the sour beer traditions of Prussia and Saxony but it is brewed like a modern pale ale. It is fermented twice: first, with *Lactobacillus* to give a balanced acidity, and then with a British strain of brewer's yeast for a smooth body. It's then dry hopped to give big juicy flavours with negligible bitterness. This is a thirst-quenching beer with a fragrant and clean taste and a sharp acidity, grapefruit flavours and no bitterness.

amarillo

SOUR

UNFILTERED. UNPASTEURISED. UNFINED.

alc 5.4% VOL.

Anchor Porter

PRODUCER: Anchor Brewing Co.

AREA OF ORIGIN: San Francisco, USA

VARIETY: Porter

ABV: 5.6%

WEBSITE: www.anchorbrewing.com

Anchor has a long proud tradition stretching back to 1871. It took the name Anchor at the end of the 19th century and it has survived fires, unexpected deaths, Prohibition, and changes in fashion and fads, to still be making some of America's finest beers and spirits. Anchor Porter became the first modern American porter when it was introduced in 1974, and it still has a huge following. It contains a blend of roasted pale, caramel, chocolate, and black malts, and is made with top-fermenting yeast. The brew is hopped at a high rate, and is naturally carbonated. The result is dark in the glass, but is bitter free and surprisingly light on the palate. This beer has lots of chocolate, liquorice, coffee, toast, and cream. There are traces of dark fruit jam, dried fruits, and cocoa beans.

Anosteké

PRODUCER: Brasserie du Pays Flamand

AREA OF ORIGIN: Blaringhem, France

VARIETY: Blonde lager

ABV: 8.0%

WEBSITE: www.brasseriedupaysflamand.com

The Brasserie du Pays Flamand was founded in November 2006 by two childhood friends, Olivier Duthoit and Mathieu Lesenne. They have brought a modern and flamboyant approach to making beer, along with a healthy respect for the environment. All ingredients are sourced locally, and spent grains are given to farmers for animal feed. Nothing is out of bounds and the duo are experimenting with ageing, maturing their beers in all types of wine, bourbon, cognac, and whisky barrels. Beers include tripels, barley wines, stouts, IPAs, and a range of sours made with blueberries, peaches, and other fruits. This beer has aromas of flowers and citrus fruits on the nose. Grapefruit and lemon are found on the palate. The finish is powerful and hoppy, with a pleasant lasting bitterness.

bière blonde artisanale
ANOSTEKE
"Le houblon fait la force"
BRASSERIE DU PAYS FLAMAND
BLARINGHEM (59) - FRANCE

Audit Ale

PRODUCER: Westerham Brewery

AREA OF ORIGIN: Westerham, England

VARIETY: Bitter

ABV: 6.2%

WEBSITE: www.westerhambrewery.co.uk

Westerham is in Kent in the South East of England, a county known as the garden of England and home to intensive hop growing. Westerham Brewery was set up by Robert Wicks in 2004 and naturally uses locally produced hops. In fact, Westerham is very much about reducing food miles in the supply chain, and is intent on reproducing many of the much loved beer flavours of the Black Eagle Brewery, which closed in 1965 after the widespread consolidation of the industry by the big brewers. Audit Ale is an award-winning strong ale made to a 1938 Black Eagle recipe. It has a fruity, hoppy, and malty nose. On the palate there is toffee and caramel, and a tangy and earthy note, with dried fruits, hops and some bitterness. It has a smooth mouthfeel and dry bitter finish. Very drinkable.

Axe Edge

PRODUCER: Buxton Brewery

AREA OF ORIGIN: Buxton, England

VARIETY: IPA

ABV: 6.8%

WEBSITE: www.buxtonbrewery.co.uk

From small acorns do big oaks grow – though, to be fair, Buxton isn't that big an oak just yet. The founders clearly remember brewing their first pale ale – 40 litres of it – on New Year's Day in 2009. It was enough to spark a passion to take their home-produced beers and bring them to a broader public.

Over the following months, recipes were tweaked, altered, thrown away and revived before they launched to the public. Axe Edge is a flagship beer for Buxton and was first introduced early on, in 2010. It is a tribute to American West Coast IPA beers and is a weighty 6.8% ABV. It's named after the moorland to the South and West of Buxton. This is a full flavoured, strong India Pale Ale, which is now hopped with Amarillo, Citra and Nelson Sauvin. Its complex flavours include mandarin orange, schnapps, pineapple, and juicy tropical fruits. It is warmingly alcoholic with a dry finish.

AXE
EDGE

INDIA PALE ALE

6.8% ALC / VOL

Backyard Lazy Daze

PRODUCER: Backyard Brewery

AREA OF ORIGIN: Manchester, New Hampshire, USA

VARIETY: IPA

ABV: 6.2%

WEBSITE: www.backyardbrewerynh.com

Backyard Brewery is housed in a bar. The beer is brewed by Paul St Onge, who is on a mission to create artisanally made beers for all to enjoy, in an atmosphere of friendliness, camaraderie and community outreach.

'My vision is that of a traditional English Public House – high-quality beer served in a place of community gathering where strangers, locals, regulars, and everyone in between can chat amongst themselves over a pint or two.'

Backyard Lazy Daze is an example of his passion for brewing IPA-style beers. He uses slaked wheat and oats to give the beer a full-bodied mouthfeel. Lazy Daze is double dry hopped with six different hops and hop powders at different points of conditioning. Fresh citrus, mango, and pineapple flavours burst out of the glass on the nose. On the palate there is a restrained bitterness, with lots of big hop flavours and aroma.

Bam Noire

PRODUCER: Jolly Pumpkin

AREA OF ORIGIN: Michigan, USA

VARIETY: Sour farmhouse ale

ABV: 4.5%

WEBSITE: www.jollypumpkin.com

Brewery founder Ron Jeffries and his wife have a strange sense of humour. Having planned their business for months, they were faced with coming up with a name, so they poured some beers and had a brainstorming session.

'Many great names were suggested but we kept coming back to Jolly Pumpkin,' says Ron. 'It encompassed everything we wanted to express about our brewery. Fun and quirky, all that needed adding were the last two words; "Artisan Ales", and the description of the brewery's products and mission: the creation of fantastic beers of truly outstanding artisan quality.'

They keep everything small and simple here, and focus on great beer. This sour ale is a beauty, and is enriched by two months in oak. It has the aroma of worn leather and cool autumn nights. There are notes of sweet plum and toasted raisin, hints of coffee and cacao. The finish is lingering, tart and refreshing.

Battledown Original

PRODUCER: Battledown Brewery

AREA OF ORIGIN: Charlton Kings, England

VARIETY: Chestnut beer

ABV: 4.4%

WEBSITE: www.battledownbrewery.com

Battledown Brewery produces fine beers for local public houses, hotels, restaurants and shops in the Cotswolds, and is thriving. It is now based in new premises in the exciting Dowdeswell Park development and is operating a busy 13-hectolitre (hl) brew-plant. The brewery says it is using the same techniques developed by generations of brewers …

'… so we are able to create beers that we are proud of. The methods are as old as the hills and the ingredients are as good as you can get, so the beers are unsurprisingly … well judge for yourself.'

This is a traditional English chestnut beer with a robust malty aroma and taste, giving way to a well rounded sweet mouthfeel. The caramel notes in this beer make it ideal with steaks, barbeques and curries. It is a medium-bodied deep amber beer, with malt and fruit overtones and a balancing bitterness from the hops.

Bede's Chalice

PRODUCER: Durham Brewery

AREA OF ORIGIN: Durham, England

VARIETY: Belgian Tripel

ABV: 9.0%

WEBSITE: www.durhambrewery.co.uk

Durham Brewery is the oldest brewery in Durham, which is in England's North East. It was established in 1994, and originally focused on the light-hoppy style of bitters. But it has consistently grown its portfolio of beers, and the brewery says that its head brewer ensures that all styles are made authentically, cutting no corners and constantly renewing plant and machinery for the highest quality. The origin of the 'Tripel' is unknown, but would appear to denote alcoholic strength. First used in the 1930s in association with the Trappist brewery Westmalle, the term now refers to a strong pale ale. This is a smooth, sweetish, luscious and fruity experience. The peach and orange notes of the malt base are enhanced by the judicious use of a single American hop, centennial.

Beyond Modus IV

PRODUCER: The Wild Beer Co

AREA OF ORIGIN: Evercreech, England

VARIETY: Sour aged red ale

ABV: 8.0%

WEBSITE: www.wildbeerco.com

The Wild Beer Co has put together a portfolio of excellent and unusual beers, and any of them could have been featured in these pages. But this beer particularly appealed.

The team behind the company sets out to make some of the world's oldest beer styles on contemporary equipment. It gives a local twist by using wild yeast harvested from a nearby orchard, and foraging for local ingredients.

Beyond Modus IV is an annual release based on the brewery's flagship beer Modus Operandi, which is described as a sour red ale, aged in ex-red wine and bourbon barrels. Modus IV is further aged in an assortment of unusual casks to make a final product that is complex and rich in flavours. Expect to taste sour cherry, red wine and balsamic.

Bitter & Twisted

PRODUCER: Harviestoun Brewery

AREA OF ORIGIN: Edinburgh, Scotland

VARIETY: Golden ale

ABV: 4.2%

WEBSITE: www.harviestoun.com

It's hard to believe that at the turn of the Millennium Scotland was still in the dark ages when it came to beer. To the casual eye it was a cask ale desert. Scratch under the surface, though, and Harviestoun had started making great beer as long ago as 1983. Now it enjoys iconic status and is at the forefront of innovation. There's a version of Bitter & Twisted finished in gin and pinot noir casks, for instance. The brewery says this beer was named after the brewer's wife, a joke that didn't go down nearly as well as this zesty, refreshing and sessionable beer does.

Black Bishop

PRODUCER: The Durham Brewery

AREA OF ORIGIN: Durham, England

VARIETY: Stout

ABV: 4.1%

WEBSITE: www.durhambrewery.co.uk

The Durham Brewery was launched in August 1994 at the Durham Beer Festival, where it promptly won 'beer of the festival' with Celtic, an achievement that was to be repeated the following year. Founders Christine and Steve Gibbs were full-time teachers at the time, but turned to full-time brewing after a year. An adventurous bottle range is now available, from the lightest beer at 3.8% ABV to the darkest 10% ABV. Black Bishop is a stout, which in turn is a stronger style of porter. It is full-bodied and rich in coffee flavours. The big malty and full flavours suggest it is stronger than it is.

Black Grouse

PRODUCER: Allendale

AREA OF ORIGIN: Hexham, England

VARIETY: Best bitter

ABV: 4.0%

WEBSITE: www.allendalebrewery.com

Allendale is located in the North East of England in a region with a strong coal mining heritage, and has been brewing beer since 2006. The brewery is a state-of-the-art 20-barrel plant run out of a historic lead smelting mill. The brewery owners say that it is this heritage that they try to reflect in their beers. Black Grouse is a seasonal ale made with Target, Fuggles and Bramling Cross hops, and a range of different malts. The result is a lively and full tasting bitter. It's smoky, oaky and with hints of liquorice. There's chocolate on both the nose and palate. Late on there's astringency from the roasted malts, balanced nicely by the sweetness. Packed full of flavour.

Bling Bling

PRODUCER: Bridge Road Brewers

AREA OF ORIGIN: Beechworth, Australia

VARIETY: IPA

ABV: 5.8%

WEBSITE: www.bridgeroadbrewers.com.au

Bridge Road Brewers brings together two great passions of its owners – beer and pizza. The pizza comes courtesy of one of the founders, who grew up in Austria a few miles from two Northern Italian towns, and she knows what she is doing when it comes to authentic pizza. That applies to the beer, too. Bridge Road, which sells its beers in its own bar, is a study in small batch craft brewing. Bling Bling is described as a 'huge beer with all the bells and whistles' and is the brewery's take on a traditional IPA style. This has a citrusy aroma, with some tropical fruits, and wood. On the palate there are tropical fruits, some grassy bitterness and mild crisp biscuity and toffee-ish malts.

BRIDGE
ROAD
BREWERS
BEECHWORTH
BLING
BLING
IMPERIAL IPA...
flavour profile
330ml

Bluebird Premium XB

PRODUCER: Coniston Brewing Company

AREA OF ORIGIN: Coniston, England

VARIETY: Hybrid bitter

ABV: 4.2%

WEBSITE: www.conistonbrewery.com

Coniston is in the Lake District in the North West of England and The Coniston Brewing Company is nestled behind The Black Bull public house. Brewery owner Ian Bradley studied and graduated in the art of brewing and founded the Coniston Brewing Company before the current craft brewing trend, in 1995. Six beers are in regular production for distribution to 100 customer outlets. Bluebird Premium XB combines two of the great themes of ale brewing to produce something distinctive and new: a quaffable and complex English pale ale and new wave American hop variety Mount Hood, which has robust citrus aromas. This is a smooth pale ale with floral hints, light malt tones and a hoppy freshness. There are hints of caramel on the nose. The palate is a clean and crisp with a citrus hop zest. A nice mix of sweetness and bitterness late on.

Boundary Export Stout

PRODUCER: Boundary Brewery

AREA OF ORIGIN: Belfast, Northern Ireland

VARIETY: Stout

ABV: 7.0%

WEBSITE: www.boundarybrewing.coop

Boundary Brewery is a co-operative Brewery in Belfast owned and run by its members. It first opened its doors in 2014, and it is the first brewery in Northern Ireland to bring together modern American styles with the more traditional Belgian/French-style beers. In December 2014 Boundary raised £100k and welcomed 447 member-owners to the cooperative. In December 2015 it opened membership again, and raised over £160 000 to grow the brewery. There are now more than 1000 members. Export Stout is a core beer and Boundary describe it as a 'decadent badboy... to be savoured and enjoyed'. Chocolate, caramel, coffee and dried fruit combine with the roasted biscuity malt base in this beer to give a complex and smooth export stout. Also strong fruit and bitter notes.

Bracia

PRODUCER: Thornbridge Brewery

AREA OF ORIGIN: Bakewell, England

VARIETY: Dark ale

ABV: 10.0%

WEBSITE: www.thornbridgebrewery.co.uk

Situated in the small town that gave us the world famous tart, Thornbridge is an established brewery with a big reputation. Thornbridge branded beers were first brewed in early 2005 after the establishment of a 10-barrel brewery in the grounds of Thornbridge Hall. Their beers – traditional ales with a modern twist – have now won over 350 national and international awards. The company moved to a new state-of-the-art brewery and bottling line in September 2009 to meet demand and increase its range of beers. Bracia is brewed only four times a year, in limited quantities; it uses chestnut honey to produce a rich, dark, unique beer. Expect honey, coffee, fresh orange fruit peel, and chocolate on the nose. On the palate there is coffee, nuts, and liquorice. The finish is earthy and rich.

Thornbridge

THORNBRIDGE
HALL

BRACIA
Rich Dark Ale

A velvety, rich ale generously infused
with dark and bitter chestnut honey.
Aromas of cappuccino, chocolate,
fresh peel, liquorice and hazelnuts
with a little peat in the finish.

10% ABV   500ml℮

INNOVATION · PASSION · KNOWLEDGE

Broken Dream

PRODUCER: Siren Craft Brew

AREA OF ORIGIN: Finchampstead, England

VARIETY: Stout

ABV: 6.0%

WEBSITE: www.sirencraftbrew.com

What makes craft brewing so exciting is the way some brewers think of new ways to take beer to exciting places. Siren is one of seven British craft brewers involved in The International Rainbow Project, which pairs seven of the best breweries in the United Kingdom with seven of the best breweries from a chosen country or region each year. In late 2016 the draw was done with a twist, as each pairing drew two colours out, with the second being for a 2018 barrel-aged beer. In the meantime, we have this breakfast stout, which the brewer describes as 'deep and complex'. Hard to resist. You expect coffee and you get it in droves – rich black coffee, expresso strength. But this is dark and seductive, with some fine spicy notes and an earthy smokiness. Pepper on the finish, too. Full of flavour.

48

Brooklyn Lager

PRODUCER: Brooklyn Brewery

AREA OF ORIGIN: New York, USA

VARIETY: Lager

ABV: 5.2%

WEBSITE: www.brooklynbrewery.com

When it comes to quality beer, the Brooklyn Brewery is a pioneer. Brooklyn brewed its first lager in 1988 and since then it has grown into a world famous brewery – but it has always stayed close to its roots. Right from the outset the brewery skipped traditional advertising in favour of donating beer to small theatres, art galleries, performers, museums, advocacy groups and more, helping to make their work and events something special. These days the brewery supports a travelling roadshow that promotes food, drink, music and art across the world. Brooklyn Lager is a classic. It was the first release from the brewery and is still its flagship beer. It is a sweet and incredibly well balanced lager, with clean and fresh hoppy notes and late citrus notes.

Brugse Zot Blond

PRODUCER: Brouwerij De Halve Maan

AREA OF ORIGIN: Bruges, Belgium

VARIETY: Blonde pale ale

ABV: 6.0%

WEBSITE: www.halvemaan.be

Drinking this beer in the brewery's tavern overlooking the canals of Bruges gets right to the very heart of craft beer drinking. Belgian beer is, of course, what true craft beer is all about, and Brouwerij De Halve Maan is the real deal. The Maes family has been brewing beer on the Walplein in Bruges for centuries and you can trace the history of the brewery in its unique museum. Brugse Zot is a delicious blonde beer, brewed according to a unique and traditional recipe. The beer also has a brown variety that is known as Brugse Zot Dubble. Brewery De Halve Maan also brews the Brugse Bok, a seasonal beer with a malty aroma. This beer balances fruity sweetness and hoppy bitterness, and is a refreshing mix of orange and lemons. Nice spices in the finish.

Buxton Anglo-Belgique

PRODUCER: Buxton Brewery

AREA OF ORIGIN: Buxton, England

VARIETY: IPA

ABV: 6.8%

WEBSITE: www.buxtonbrewery.co.uk

Buxton Brewery now has 10 members of staff and is based in a 7000-square-foot modern building on Staden Lane, Buxton. It's custom designed and (British) built brewhouse produces around 3500 litres per brew, three times per week – a significant step up from the secondhand 800-litre plant of old.

The brewery makes upwards of 30 distinct brews of all kinds, and it has released several Belgian-style beers but Anglo-Belgique is a little different – it takes the character and distinguished history of the Belgian ale and marries it with the aroma and bitterness of the English-born IPA. This has an aroma of yeast and green apples. The taste is refreshing, with hops and malts battling each other, and a peachy and apple-like note in the mix. Strange finish with some earthy notes.

Calypso

PRODUCER: Siren Craft Brewing

AREA OF ORIGIN: Finchhampstead, England

VARIETY: Sour beer

ABV: 4.0%

WEBSITE: www.sirencraftbrew.com

This beer probably epitomises everything good about craft brewing. Siren Craft Brewing is a modern, stylish brewery in Berkshire but it is obsessive about making fine beer based on traditional recipes. And it makes beers like this one, which work on different levels. For instance, you might want to simply enjoy the zingy taste of the beer, or you might like to know that Calypso was a goddess known for her sharp tongue; this beer is a homage to this enchantress – a tart, spritz Berliner-style sour beer that is liberally dry hopped with a different single hop for each batch. And you might even want to know which hop you are drinking. And, thanks to siren, you can do that too – check out the Siren website and match the batch number to the hop. The alcoholic strength is modest by the standards of many beers in this book, but this is still in your face. Sharp and tart, this has lemon and tropical fruit riding a hoppy undercurrent.

Caribbean Chocolate Cake

PRODUCER: Siren Craft Brewing

AREA OF ORIGIN: Finchhampstead, England

VARIETY: Stout

ABV: 7.4%

WEBSITE: www.sirencraftbrew.com

More proof that Siren is thinking outside the box. This beer is a collaboration with Cigar City, a brewery based in Tampa, Florida, which according to Siren has consistently been producing great beers since opening its doors in 2008. It particularly specialises in the use of wood in its beers and Siren wanted to capture this:

'... instead of putting the beer in wood, we put wood in the beer.'

The resulting stout is packed with experimental hop varieties, and a lot of Cyprus wood. 'This beer is a true example of what can happen if you leave two hugely creative brewers with complete free reign – it's the ultimate anti-recession blockbuster!' says the brewery.

This has 'an impressive roster of flavours such as orange, dark chocolate, coconut, tamarind, lemon, coffee and even vanilla wafers,' says the brewery. 'It is one of the most complex and interesting creations we have made.'

Casey Saison

PRODUCER: Casey Brewing & Blending

AREA OF ORIGIN: Colorado, USA

VARIETY: Farmhouse ale

ABV: 5.5%

WEBSITE: www.caseybrewing.com

Casey Brewing & Blending was created by Troy Casey in 2013 after years of experimenting with oak barrel ageing using wild yeasts and bacteria. All of Casey's ingredients are from Colorado, with the idea of bringing old-world brewing techniques to the modern-day consumer.

'Time is one of the most important elements to us, as the barrel ageing process creates flavours that are impossible to create any other way,' he says. Saison is an old-fashioned style of beer, fermented in open oak barrel fermenters and then further aged in barrels.

The result is a citrusy, dry, effervescent and tart beer.

The aroma is a pleasant mixture of lemon, lime, dried grass, gentle spices, and a bit of pepper. Acidic and tart on the palate, with more citrus fruits, and a tart and sharp finish.

SAISON

ALE AGED IN OAK BARRELS

750 ML

1 PT. 9.4 FL. OZ.

6.5% ALC. BY VOL.

BREWED AND BOTTLED BY CASEY BREWING AND BLENDING LLC
GLENWOOD SPRINGS, COLORADO

Celis White

PRODUCER: Celis Brewery

AREA OF ORIGIN: Texas, USA

VARIETY: White beer

ABV: 5.0%

WEBSITE: www.celisbeers.com

Few beer brands have such a dramatic back story as Celis White. The witbier style of beer goes back centuries, but was almost extinct in 1966 when milkman Pierre Celis started brewing it again. By 1985 he was making 300 000 barrels a year but his Hoegaarden brewery burned down and, as he was under insured, he was forced to sell his beer brand to Interbrew, now Anheuser Busch. Pierre relocated to Austin, Texas, where he founded a new brewery and brewed Celis White to an age-old recipe. But after Pierre died the brand name was sold and was shunted from company to company. In 2017 Pierre's daughter, Christine Celis, acquired the name again, and her brewery opened in Austin in July 2017.

This beer is full-bodied and flavoursome, with waves of lemons and spices. It's light and soft on the palate, due to some fruity, lightly acid notes.

Clogwyn Gold

PRODUCER: Bragdy Conwy Brewery

AREA OF ORIGIN: Conwy, Wales

VARIETY: Mild pale ale

ABV: 3.6%

WEBSITE: conwybrewery.co.uk

Using the naturally soft water coming off the mountains of Snowdonia, Bragdy Conwy Brewery produces a range of cask and bottle conditioned ales. The brewery makes four styles of beer: Conwy ales, which are popular ales available all year designed to have broad appeal; Seasonal ales; West Coast ales, which showcase modern beer styles; and small batch brews – limited-edition brews that try something new each month. Clogwyn Gold is from the first category and it is a thirst quencher. The brewery says it goes well with a curry after a day's mountain walking. Tropical fruit aromas are followed by sweet malts and a gentle bitter aftertaste. Bready and tasty for a beer of this strength.

Coolship Cerise

PRODUCER: Allagash Brewing Company

AREA OF ORIGIN: Portland, USA

VARIETY: Coolship

ABV: 8.1%

WEBSITE: www.allagash.com

Allagash Brewing Company has been brewing in
Portland since 1995 and is dedicated to crafting fine
Belgian-inspired beers. In 2007 it started brewing a
style known as Coolship. These brews are crafted using a
traditional Belgian method of spontaneous fermentation.
Hot, unfermented wort is cooled overnight using
outside air temperature in a traditional, large shallow
pan known as a 'coolship'. During the cooling process,
naturally occurring microflora from the air inoculates
the beer. It is transferred into French oak wine barrels,
where the entire fermentation and ageing for one to
three years takes place. It is aged on cherries for six
months, in oak wine barrels. The beer is pale red in
colour with cherry and spice in the aroma. Cherry,
oak and spice punctuate the flavour of this tart beer.

COOLSHIP
cerise

ale aged in oak barrels
with cherries

ALLAGASH BREWING COMPANY

OPEN CAUTIOUSLY: CONTENTS UNDER PRESSURE

8.1% Alc. by Vol. • 12.7 fl oz (375 ml)

Crafty Dan 13 Guns

PRODUCER: Daniel Thwaites

AREA OF ORIGIN: Blackburn, England

VARIETY: American IPA

ABV: 5.5%

WEBSITE: www.thwaitesbeers.co.uk

Crafty Dan indeed. Daniel Thwaites has been brewing for more than 200 years and it has always maintained its reputation for great quality, no matter how big it has become and how many pubs, inns, hotels and spas it now owns.

The company says it has flourished by remaining steadfastly faithful to Daniel's original principles and has attempted to stay independent and customer-focused. What better way to do so than to make fine craft beer, and to set up an experimental microbrewery to do so? 13 Guns is an IPA made with American hops. It has the aroma of toffee, peach and mango. On the palate there are bold malty notes, toffee and Garibaldi biscuits, grapefruit and tangerine. Very rich and full.

Cross Bones

PRODUCER: Heavy Seas

AREA OF ORIGIN: Baltimore, USA

VARIETY: IPA

ABV: 4.5%

WEBSITE: www.hsbeer.com

Cross Bones is Heavy Seas's first new beer to be available all year round since 2003. The plan was to create a perfect session IPA that would satisfy the hoppiest of hop heads and maximise flavour, while not creating something too strong to put drinkers under the table. They have succeeded. This has a taste and flavour that suggests a heavier strength than 4.5%. It is bursting with floral and citrus notes and has a strong malt backbone to support all of that hoppy goodness. The recipe includes six different malts and a secret combination of hops, and the result is a full-bodied, flavoursome and smooth beer.

Cuvee de Tomme

PRODUCER: The Lost Abbey

AREA OF ORIGIN: California, USA

VARIETY: Brown ale

ABV: 11.0%

WEBSITE: www.lostabbey.com

The Lost Abbey is one of America's most remarkable craft breweries. It is the creation of brother and sister team Vince and Gina Marsaglia and brewer Tomme Arthur, who set out to make a range of outstanding beers based on the tasty treats made by Belgian Trappist monks. Distribution has now expanded to major cities and metropolitan areas throughout the USA. Cuvee de Tomme is a massive brown ale made from four fermentable sugars including malted barley, raisins, candy sugar and sour cherries. It is fully fermented before being matured in bourbon barrels for one year along with the sour cherries and wild yeast that the barrels are inoculated with.

De Ranke XXX-Bitter

PRODUCER: Brouwerij de Ranke

AREA OF ORIGIN: Belgium

VARIETY: Bitter

ABV: 6.0%

WEBSITE: www.deranke.be

De Ranke Brewery is a partnership between brewer Nino Bacelle and beer enthusiast Guido Devos, and the name refers to the vines on which hops grow. The first launch was a Christmas ale followed by XX, in 1996. And since then a series of beers have been released. XXX-Bitter is a variation on the existing XX-Bitter, with an additional 50% more hops included in the recipe. It is a full-bodied bitter beer. It's made with Brewers Gold and Hallertau Mittelfrüh hops, and the large amount of aroma-hops makes this beer taste smoother than XX.

Dead Pony Club

PRODUCER: Brewdog

AREA OF ORIGIN: Ellon, Scotland

VARIETY: Pale ale

ABV: 3.8%

WEBSITE: www.brewdog.com

If you have any doubts about Brewdog's credentials as craft beer's attack dogs against bland corporate brewing, then look no further than co-founder James Watt's attack on the Portman Group after it banned its Dead Pony Club packaging due to what it said was 'inappropriate association with bravado and immoderate consumption'. Watt said: 'Unfortunately, the Portman Group is a gloomy gaggle of killjoy jobsworths, funded by navel-gazing international drinks giants.'

Dead Pony Club is an American-style pale ale with lemon and lime zest and a big hoppy flavour. Remember, children, to drink it responsibly so as not to upset the authorities.

Dennis Hopp'r

PRODUCER: Mondo Brewing Company

AREA OF ORIGIN: London, England

VARIETY: IPA

ABV: 5.3%

WEBSITE: www.mondobrewingcompany.com

Mondo means 'world' in Italian and the founders of this brewery thought that it was an appropriate name because they take a global approach to brewing and are influenced by a wide range of different cultures. The brewery was founded by Todd Matteson and Thomas Palmer, who began as home brewers but committed to learning to brew professionally. They made their first beer in March 2015.

Dennis Hopp'r is one of a number of beers with playful and fun names, and is made with three grains and Citra and Vic Secret hops to maximise the fruity flavours in the beer. There is an appealing bitterness to this beer, too.

Ein Stein

PRODUCER: Lymestone Brewery

AREA OF ORIGIN: Stone, England

VARIETY: Continental-style pale ale

ABV: 5.0%

WEBSITE: www.lymestonebrewery.co.uk

Stone is a small town in Staffordshire, England, and the Lymestone Brewery is a family microbrewing business that keeps the region's brewing traditions alive. Founder and director Ian Bradford is in charge of brewing, and he has now been joined by his daughter Sarah. Ian's wife Viv keeps the ship steady by handling sales, marketing and accounts. The brewery keeps bees on its roof, and some of this honey is used in the brewery's Stone Brood beer.

Ein Stein uses pale Maris Otter malts and German hops to make a refreshing and drinkable pale ale. There are notes of banana and cloves on the nose, while the taste is malty and hoppy, with a pleasant bitterness. Ein Stein can be found within a radius of about 50 miles from the brewery and in the brewery's two brewery taps in Stone.

Engine Vein

PRODUCER: Cheshire Brewhouse

AREA OF ORIGIN: Congleton, England

VARIETY: Copper ale

ABV: 4.2%

WEBSITE: www.cheshirebrewhouse.co.uk

Cheshire Brewhouse is in England's North West and is home to lifetime brewer and publican's son Shane Swindells, who has worked as an engineer in big commercial breweries and has developed his love of craft beer with his own brews. Having his own brewery was a long held aim, and he made a point of gaining as much knowledge from the many beer people he met over the years. Engine Vein is named after an ancient copper mine in the locality.

It is a traditional but finely made bitter, with a biscuity, grainy taste, and a lovely hop note. Described by the makers as both traditional and contemporary.

Ensorcelled

PRODUCER: The Rare Barrel

AREA OF ORIGIN: Berkeley, USA

VARIETY: Sour beer

ABV: 6.2%

WEBSITE: www.therarebarrel.com

The Rare Barrel makes sour beer, which is a style of beer produced by a unique and involved fermentation and ageing process that cannot be replicated in any other food or beverage. The brewery is dedicated to the conditioning of barrel-aged sour beers.

Ensorcelled – great name – is flavoured with cherries and has notes of smooth dark chocolate paired with tart raspberries. It is brewed each year and it varies from batch to batch, but the brewery reports that the recent version is richer and more intense than ever. It is, says the brewery, luscious like a chocolate mousse topped with a raspberry glaze – a dessert you can sip.

Falkon Kamsot

PRODUCER: Pivovar Falkon

AREA OF ORIGIN: Zatec, Czech Republic

VARIETY: Stout

ABV: 6.6%

WEBSITE: www.pivofalkon.cz

Pivovar Falkon is a modern brewery in a country with a long and proud heritage of beer making. The brewery was founded in 2012 in the beer-rich region of Bohemia by Jakub Veselỹ, a nineteen-year-old who had started brewing at the age of 12 – when he didn't even like the taste of beer. When he graduated with a degree in brewing technology he couldn't get a job, so he set up his own brewery – with no money and no beer. Falkon Kamsot shows how far he's come – it's a sweet stout with coffee, caramel and rich fruity notes. Smooth and enjoyable.

Farmer's Reserve Blueberry

PRODUCER: Almanac Beer Company

AREA OF ORIGIN: California, USA

VARIETY: Sour blonde

ABV: 7.0%

WEBSITE: www.almanacbeer.com

The Almanac Beer Company was founded in 2010 by Jesse Friedman and Damian Fagan, two friends who had brewed small batches of beer in their respective San Francisco apartments for years, while developing a passion for crafting unique and unusual beers unavailable commercially. It is a farm-to-barrel brewing operation and is proud of it. Only the best locally-sourced fruit is used and blended into beers inspired by the great brewing traditions of the world. The brewery's sour blonde base beer is aged with blueberries from Northern California. The aim is to blend rich fruit flavours with refreshing tartness. This beer has a luscious purple hue.

Farmhouse Red

PRODUCER: La Sirène

AREA OF ORIGIN: Melbourne, Australia

VARIETY: Red ale

ABV: 6.0%

WEBSITE: www.lasirene.com.au

La Sirène set out with the intention of making modern day artisanal farmhouse-style beers with character and identity but, say the brewers, it quickly evolved into a life-long obsession. They originally brewed in the Victorian Highlands, but are now based in their farmhouse brewery next door to the Darebin Creek & National Park in inner-city Melbourne.

'We consider ourselves "farmhouse free stylers", as well as mixed, wild and spontaneous fermentation yeast wranglers and alchemists!', they say.

Farmhouse Red is a rustic-style red ale brewed with five different Belgian specialty malts along with fresh rose buds, hibiscus and dandelions, to provide a provincial farmhouse-style Belgian ale experience.

First World Problems

PRODUCER: Stewart Brewing

AREA OF ORIGIN: Edinburgh, Scotland

VARIETY: Belgian IPA

ABV: 6.2%

WEBSITE: www.stewartbrewing.co.uk

Stewart Brewing is an independent brewery, founded in Edinburgh by Steve and Jo Stewart in 2004. They started off with just the two of them on the payroll, making three cask beers. They introduced more experimental beers, started to bottle their beer and sell it in kegs, but by 2010 they had run out of space and couldn't keep up with demand. So they invested in a new 50 hl Bavarian brew kit and housed it in a new brewery. The name First World Problems is tongue-in-cheek but this is a mighty serious beer, made by experienced and keen home brewer James Hardcare, sponsored by the brewery. First World Problems balances maltiness, bitterness and fruitiness in equal measure. Very good indeed.

FMB 101

PRODUCER: Figueroa Mountain Brewing Co.

AREA OF ORIGIN: California, USA

VARIETY: Blonde ale

ABV: 4.8%

WEBSITE: www.figmtnbrew.com

Absolute proof that craft brewing has little to do with size. This brewery has grown rapidly over its lifetime, but it's still making beer the same way as it always did. Figueroa Mountain Brewing Co. was founded by father-and-son team Jim and Jaime Dietenhofer in 2010. The company has become one of the fastest-growing craft breweries in America, and now has a staff of over 200, which they affectionately call the #FigFam.

101 is named after the highway where the Californian coast meets its mountains, and this is a light, refreshing ale with notes of malt and honey.

Foundation 11

PRODUCER: CREW Republic

AREA OF ORIGIN: Munich, Germany

VARIETY: German pale ale

ABV: 5.6%

WEBSITE: www.crewrepublic.de

CREW Republic is the creation of two home brewing friends who gave up their jobs to make great beer and through perseverance, hard work, and a considerable amount of talent, built up a business that has seen them open their own brewery in 2015. Foundation 11 was the brewers' first release, from the very early days of home brewing, the result of a lot of experimentation, and it has sold well ever since. It is a German-style pale ale. It's got a strong hoppiness to it, but there are toasted oats and citrus fruits in the mix, and a long, bitter and dry finish.

Fraoch Ale

PRODUCER: Williams Bros. Brewing Co.

AREA OF ORIGIN: Alloa, Scotland

VARIETY: Heather ale

ABV: 5.0%

WEBSITE: www.williamsbrosbrew.com

The story goes that the recipe for Leanne Fraoch was given to Bruce Williams by a strange woman who came into the family home-brew shop. The recipe was for a beer made with heather, which grows plentifully in Scotland. Hops don't, so the idea of a distinctly Scottish beer product was highly attractive. Demand for Bruce's beer was huge, so the first batch sold out quickly. Bruce teamed up with his brother, Scott, to pre-sell the next batch. Now seasonal heather is harvested and frozen to ensure year-round supply. Fraoch is genuinely different. It has an aroma that is both floral and smoky, and it has a strong malty taste and a spicy, herbal finish provided by hops and heather.

Freedom Amber Rye

PRODUCER: Freedom Brewery

AREA OF ORIGIN: Abbots Bromley, England

VARIETY: Amber rye lager

ABV: 4.7%

WEBSITE: www.freedombrewery.com

Freedom is a little different to many of the microbreweries featured in this book because it was at the forefront of a move to get a reappraisal of the British relationship with lager. The Campaign for Real Ale – the clue's in the name – was content to embrace Belgian and Continental lagers but wasn't so sure about British lager. That's changed thanks to companies such as Freedom. The brewery is also high-tech and state-of-the-art. It's still craft brewing, though, and here's why: Amber Rye is a dark lager with rye malt and Centennial and Cascade hops. It has a full, spicy taste and is anything but bland.

Friday

PRODUCER: Martin House Brewing Company

AREA OF ORIGIN: Fort Worth, USA

VARIETY: IPA

ABV: 6.0%

WEBSITE: www.martinhousebrewing.com

This brewery is named after one of the founders and partly because of the purple martin, a native Texan bird that nests in shared 'houses'. Purple martins are known for their aerial acrobatics, and Texans love watching them catch all their food in flight. The brewery was founded in the original Martin home garage and ever since then there has been an emphasis on the fun side of brewing and the pure love of it. Friday is brewed with a hefty amount of Mosaic, Chinook, Amarillo, and Simcoe hops. The brewery says: 'It's dank, hoppy, and juicy – this beer is a flavor bomb!'

Funk

PRODUCER: Bad Seed Brewery

AREA OF ORIGIN: Malton, England

VARIETY: Sour

ABV: 5.5%

WEBSITE: www.badseedbrewery.com

Bad Seed is a small microbrewery founded in Malton, North Yorkshire, in 2013 by two home brewers passionate about the beers they made. Bad Seed uses innovative recipes and high-quality ingredients. Within two years they had moved to bigger premises and are now renowned for handcrafted, full flavour beers. Bad Seed has a wide range of beers, all unfined and unfiltered. Funk is a keg-barrel-aged, barrel-fermented sour. The primary fermentation takes place in a wooden barrel, then it is aged in a number of barrels with *Brettanomyces*, *Pediococcus* and *Lactobacillus*, before being blended back to give a complex, rich and distinct sour character. This is a sharp, fresh and clean beer, with drying citrus notes. Rich, full and complex, with hoppy sourness and a lingering finish.

Gadds' No 3

PRODUCER: The Ramsgate Brewery

AREA OF ORIGIN: Ramsgate, England

VARIETY: Pale ale

ABV: 5.0%

WEBSITE: www.ramsgatebrewery.co.uk

'Our Brewery began life in the back of a Ramsgate boozer full of louts and ne'er-do-wells, back in 2002,' say the founders of Ramsgate Brewery, with tongue firmly in cheek. 'In 2006 we purchased a big shed and set-up again bigger, better and bolder than before, brewing fresh, tasty, local ale for fresh, tasty locals. And it worked. It worked so well we've got our own website now and we're chuffed.' Indeed they have. And they have Gadds' No 3, a simple but top-quality pale ale, made with world class hops from Kent in the South East of England, local barley and Kent sunshine.

Gentleman's Wit

PRODUCER: Camden Town Brewery

AREA OF ORIGIN: London, England

VARIETY: White beer

ABV: 4.3%

WEBSITE: www.camdenbrewery.com

'Lager has a bad reputation but everyone drinks it. Just like those bands that everyone listens to but would never dare admit. At Camden Town, we love lager. Love. It.'

That's some statement of intent, but Camden Town Brewery takes its lager very seriously indeed, aiming for distinctive and flavoursome beers. Everyone who joins the business goes to Bamberg within their first year to experience first-hand where the brewery gets its house Pilsner malt from. Camden Town does more than just straight lager, though. Gentleman's Wit is a white beer that is based on the said Pilsner malt, but with wheat too. It's a highly palatable and refreshing beer – and a match for the best of European white beers. This is a soft and fruity mouth-coating beer, with notes of fresh oranges and lemons, some coriander and other spices, and a sweet wheat finish.

Ghost Ship

PRODUCER: Adnams

AREA OF ORIGIN: Southwold, England

VARIETY: Pale ale

ABV: 4.5%

WEBSITE: www.adnams.co.uk

Based in the Suffolk coastal town of Southwold, Adnams has grown into some business, with pubs, hotels, retail outlets and a distillery making award-winning spirits all part of the offering these days. The emphasis has always been on top quality, and the company hasn't forgotten that its roots are in beer. Inspired by the Bell pub at nearby Warbeswick, and the treacherous sandbanks that have led to countless wrecks along the Suffolk coast, this is a very drinkable pale ale made with a range of American hop varieties. It has a refreshing citrus and biscuity taste and is perfectly balanced between alcoholic bite and drinkability.

Ginormous

PRODUCER: Gigantic Brewing Company

AREA OF ORIGIN: Portland, USA

VARIETY: Imperial IPA

ABV: 8.8%

WEBSITE: www.giganticbrewing.com

Gigantic Brewing Company is a partnership between brewers Ben Love and Van Havig, and it is on a mission to question brewing convention and to make beers that bring new flavours to its drinkers. Many of the brewery's creations are only brewed once, and there is a sense that the brewery never stands still. At the heart of what they do are a number of flavoursome and balanced Imperial IPAs. Ginormous is made in batches, and each varies, but the aim is to make ever hoppier quality beers. They are perfected to a secret recipe in the brewery's testing facility, and a new batch is released every seven or eight weeks.

Gonzo Imperial Porter

PRODUCER: Flying Dog

AREA OF ORIGIN: USA

VARIETY: Porter

ABV: 9.2%

WEBSITE: www.flyingdogbrewery.com

The Gonzo is a reference to Hunter S. Thompson, who was friends with Flying Dog creator George Stranahan. Ralph Steadman designed the Flying Dog beer labels, and they're ace. The name Flying Dog is a reference to a historic climb of K2 in 1993 that Stranahan made. It's a long story; see www.georgestrnahan.com and be amazed. Stranahan started a brew pub in 1990 and a brewery four years later. Gonzo Imperial Porter is as big and feisty as the man it's dedicated to, with vanilla, chocolate, coffee and malt flavours and a big bite from the strength. Goes well with chili and barbecue foods, apparently.

Goose IPA

PRODUCER: Goose Island

AREA OF ORIGIN: Chicago, USA

VARIETY: IPA

ABV: 5.9%

WEBSITE: www.gooseisland.com

Goose Island is one of the legends of the craft brewing industry. It was one of the few brewers swimming against the corporate tide as long ago as 1988, the brainchild of John Hall, who had visited Europe and tasted an array of exciting beers. By 1995 the company had moved into a bigger brewery and now produces beer on a much larger scale, though it stays true to its original ideals. This is one of the brewery's most feted beers and is now world famous. It is made with four different hop types, and is fruity, hoppy, and malty in equal measure.

Green Devil

PRODUCER: Oakham Ales

AREA OF ORIGIN: Peterborough, England

VARIETY: IPA

ABV: 6.0%

WEBSITE: www.oakhamales.com

Oakham is a town in East Leicestershire – or Rutland as the locals prefer to call it – but the brewery is no longer there; it has moved East to the city of Peterborough. When the current brewhouse opened in 2006, original brewer John Wood was brought in to cut the symbolic lock and chain as part of the opening ceremony. The brewery is situated in a large city gastro pub and makes a range of award-winning beers. Green Devil is a beauty. It was first released in 2011, and is the big brother of the brewery's award-winning Citra. It has picked up countless awards since. This is a refreshing and smooth beer with the flavours of lots of orchard and tropical fruits. Crisp and clean.

Gueuze Tilquin à l'Ancienne

PRODUCER: Gueuzerie Tilquin

AREA OF ORIGIN: Bierghes, Belgium

VARIETY: Gueuze

ABV: 6.4%

WEBSITE: www.gueuzerietilquin.be

Gueuze beer is a specific form of lambic beer, and lambic beer is one of the weirdest, wildest and oldest styles of beer in the world. Lambic beer is naturally fermented by airborne wild yeasts. The result is sour, tart and strange, and tastes nothing like beer. Gueuze is a mix of old and young lambics, matured for two to three years in casks, and then blended to produce what has been called the 'Champagne of beer' – but it could easily be described as marmite. This one is from the only gueuzerie in Wallonia and, suffice to say, it is an extremely good example of the style. Tread carefully though.

Oude

GUEUZE
TILQUIN

À l'ancienne

Product of Belgium

Guldenberg

PRODUCER: Brouwerij de Ranke

AREA OF ORIGIN: Dottenijs, Belgium

VARIETY: Tripel

ABV: 8.0%

WEBSITE: www.deranke.be

The partnership behind this stylish and quaint brewery have brewing roots stretching back to the 1980s, but this brewery site was opened as De Ranke in 2005. This beer was first created 11 years earlier, and in the first year 9000 litres of it were sold. It has stayed in the brewery's production ever since. Guldenberg is a high-fermenting, balanced bitter beer. The origin of the name comes from the former Guldenberg Abbey, which is in the town of Wevelgem, where monks used to make beer, and where one of the brewers was born. It is described as a full-bodied abbey beer that balances between sweet and bitter.

Gunnamatta Earl Grey IPA

PRODUCER: The Yeastie Boys

AREA OF ORIGIN: Wellington, New Zealand

VARIETY: IPA

ABV: 6.5%

WEBSITE: www.yeastieboys.co.nz

Great company name, and the duo behind this company have the motto 'making irreverent ales, made for all beer loving folk', so, unsurprisingly, there's a fun element to their beers. Stu McKinlay and Sam Possenniskie describe themselves as creative director and directive creator respectively, and as 'beer activists' who stay ahead of the game 'by being food and drink lovers first.'

Gunnamatta Earl Grey IPA is made with significant amounts of Blue Flower tea to create a beer that has a lemon and floral nose, and a citrusy taste with a very long drying finish. The duo describe it as a 'unique new world pale ale with a decidedly old world twist'.

Halcyon

PRODUCER: Thornbridge Brewery

AREA OF ORIGIN: Bakewell, England

VARIETY: IPA

ABV: 7.4%

WEBSITE: www.thornbridgebrewery.co.uk

Thornbridge is really a tale of two breweries. Its original Hall brewery, within the grounds of Thornbridge Hall, was perfect for establishing the new beers, making high quality beer using a traditional infusion mash ale system. It also provided a platform for experimentation and for barrel-aged and premium bottled products. Indeed, so successful was it that the brewers had to move to expand. The new Riverside Brewery, in Bakewell, is perfect for innovation and for developing beers through fantastic brewing and quality control.

Halcyon is another IPA but this one is at a higher strength and is bursting with intense pineapple, grapefruit, lemon zest and pine hop flavours.

Hardknott Azimuth

PRODUCER: Hardknott Brewery

AREA OF ORIGIN: Millon, England

VARIETY: IPA

ABV: 5.8%

WEBSITE: www.hardknott.com

Cumbria, in the north west of England, is where you'll find the Lake District, as well as some seriously scary mountain walks. It's a stunning area to make beer. Hardknott is named after a notorious pass that the brewery was at the foot of. It has now moved to another beauty spot at the foot of Black Combe Fell, in the South West part of the Lake District. Azimuth is the brewery's exceptional IPA, and while batches vary, the search for the perfect hop combination is relentless. The most recent version is described as floral, with apricot notes on the nose and peach skins and fruity bitterness on the palate.

Headless

PRODUCER: Red Willow

AREA OF ORIGIN: Macclesfield, England

VARIETY: Pale ale

ABV: 3.9%

WEBSITE: www.redwillowbrewery.com

Red Willow has been a success story ever since it was launched by Toby and Caroline McKenzie in 2010. The brewery started out making a beer called Directionless, which was sold at pubs across Macclesfield. Within two years the couple had brought another brewer on board and expanded, and late in that year Ageless became the brewery's first bottled beer. Further expansions now mean that the brewery has new premises, a canning line, a staff of 12, and a capacity of some 80 barrels a week. Headless is an easy drinking session pale ale. It's described as light, refreshing and with grain and cereal notes, as well as some citrus.

Heart & Soul

PRODUCER: Vocation Brewery

AREA OF ORIGIN: Hebden Bridge, England

VARIETY: IPA

ABV: 4.4%

WEBSITE: www.vocationbrewery.com

Vocation & Co is a bar in the West Yorkshire town of
Hebden Bridge, and it's a smart and stylish venue that
serves a mouthwatering selection of taco dishes to
accompany your beer experience. Many brewers are
embracing cans these days, and nobody has a finer
looking selection of canned beers than Vocation.
The taste of its Heart & Soul matches the high-class
packaging. It has the full flavour of an IPA but at a
sessionable strength. There are big flavours from
American West Coast hops and a fruit bowl of
flavours, including mango, pineapple, grapefruit and
tropical fruits. It really works and is quite irresistible.

VOCATION BREWERY

ESTD. MMXV

HEART
& SOUL

FRUITY   TROPICAL   AROMA

SESSION IPA 4.4%

Hibernation

PRODUCER: Big Hug Brewery

AREA OF ORIGIN: London, England

VARIETY: IPA

ABV: 5.2%

WEBSITE: www.bighugbrewing.com

As the name might suggest, there's an element of hippness to London-based brewers Big Hug. They describe at length on their website how they set up the brewery with friends, to create great and full-flavoured beers. They have linked their beer operation to the environmentally-friendly Green Squares loyalty and reward scheme by which if you buy a beer you are given a square of rainforest, which will be protected for 12 months. Hibernation is the brewery's flagship beer and is a hybrid style of beer popular in the United States. The brewers have reduced the bitterness, and the strength means it tastes like a full-bodied IPA, but a high wheat content gives it a wheat beer aspect. It has a pleasant aroma, with a fine intensity. Nice fresh bitterness and a semi-dry ending. Yeast, fruity, malty, herbal and some pine in the flavour. Definite wheat beer characteristics and refreshing citrus.

BIG HUG BREWING

B

HIBERNATION

5.2%

WHITE IPA

Hof ten Dormaal Saison

PRODUCER: Brouwerij Hof ten Dormaal

AREA OF ORIGIN: Tildonk, Belgium

VARIETY: Farmhouse ale

ABV: 5.5%

WEBSITE: www.hoftendormaal.com

The brewery at Hof ten Dormaal was set up on a farm to make the business more financially viable, and it has continued to make great beer even though the brewery was completely destroyed by fire in January 2015, reopening in 2016. Since then the brewery has experimented with sour beers, and saison beers like this one. This is a farmhouse ale and is as traditional as beer making gets. It is made just with hops and grain and was originally created to be drunk during and after working in the fields. Thus it is highly refreshing and drinkable with a slightly sour taste, and a lime-like tartness

Hop Gun

PRODUCER: Funky Buddha Brewery

AREA OF ORIGIN: Boca Raton, USA

VARIETY: IPA

ABV: 7.0%

WEBSITE: www.funkybuddhabrewery.com

As the name might imply, Funky Buddha is arguably to beer what Heston Blumenthal is to food. It was founded in 2010 in Boca Raton, Florida, and is committed to producing bold craft beers that marry culinary-inspired ingredients with time-honoured techniques. It makes beers with flavours you wouldn't normally associate with beer; such as peanut butter and jelly, which it says smells and tastes like fresh roasted peanuts and fruity berry jam. The brewery is South Florida's largest craft microbrewery, and Hop Gun is one of the brewery's flagship beers. It is like all Funky Buddha beers – huge in flavour, with big hoppy grapefruit and pineapple.

Hop Hog

PRODUCER: Feral Brewing Co.

AREA OF ORIGIN: Baskerville, Australia

VARIETY: IPA

ABV: 5.8%

WEBSITE: www.feralbrewing.com.au

If you're only going to visit one website mentioned in this book, make sure it's this one. Suffice to say that the folk behind Feral are a bit nuts. 'We like our beers like we like our metaphors: heavy,' they say. 'And let's be clear. We aren't a craft brewery, we're a brewery; we don't brew craft beer, we brew beer. We don't care how others label it, we just want you to enjoy it for what it isn't: session IPAs, XPAs, hijacked corporate mumbo jumboism-isms.' Hop Hog is an American-style IPA and is a delightful mix of hops, malt and citrus notes.

Hopfenstopfer Citra Ale

PRODUCER: Häffner Brauerei

AREA OF ORIGIN: Bad Rappenau, Germany

VARIETY: Pale ale

ABV: 5.1%

WEBSITE: www.brauerei-haeffner.de

Bad Rappenau is a pretty and relaxed spa town in Germany and this brewery is part of a hotel, guest house and restaurant with a long history stretching back to the 19th century. They have been making beer here for more than a century, too, and they're very good at it. The perfect way to enjoy this pale ale is in the evening on the sun terrace of the restaurant – but it's available by mail order too.

Hopfenstopfer Citra Ale is an American-style pale ale that is light and easy to drink. Tangerine and orange are to the fore, and the finish is hoppy and bitter.

Howling Pils

PRODUCER: Howling Hops

AREA OF ORIGIN: London, England

VARIETY: Bohemian Pilsner

ABV: 4.6%

WEBSITE: www.howlinghops.co.uk

There's a clue in the name – the aim of this London-based microbrewery is to create an ever-changing range of characterful and uncompromising beers. It started life in the basement of Hackney's first brew pub, in 2011, but moved to its current home, a spacious victorian warehouse, in 2015. The brewery is on one side of the room and a bar and drinking area served directly by 10 beer tanks is on the other. This is based on the Czech style of Pils and is fresh, crisp and clean – and very more-ish. It is one of several beers being bottled by the brewery.

Imperial Extra Double Stout

PRODUCER: Harveys

AREA OF ORIGIN: Lewes, England

VARIETY: Stout

ABV: 9.0%

WEBSITE: www.harveys.org.uk

One of England's most respected brewers has built its reputation on making unpasteurised cask ales with the finest ingredients and ensuring that they are kept in perfect condition wherever they are served. But while traditional, the brewery has made some excellent seasonal and bottled beers. Imperial Extra Double Stout is a weighty 9% proof, and not for the faint-hearted. It is based on a 19th-century recipe for a beer exported to Russia, and it is a weird and wacky concoction that is sweet, sour and spicy. It has picked up a string of awards and occupies a unique space in the world of beer.

The style "IMPERIAL RUSSIAN STOUT" and the name "ALBERT LE COQ" are synonymous. In the early 1800's the Belgian A. LE COQ exported Imperial Stout from England to Russia and the Baltic area.

IMPERIAL EXTRA DOUBLE STOUT

ДЕПАРТАМЕНТЪ ТОРГОВЛИ И МАНУФ

ВДАНЬ Ѣ МАНУФАКТУРЪ

London.

PRODUCT OF THE UNITED KINGDOM

Jaipur

PRODUCER: Thornbridge Brewery

AREA OF ORIGIN: Bakewell, England

VARIETY: IPA

ABV: 5.9%

WEBSITE: www.thornbridgebrewery.co.uk

Success has been rapid for Thornbridge. The brewery opened in 2005 in the grounds of Thornbridge Hall, and from the outset it aimed to produce top quality beers by taking traditional beer styles and giving them a modern twist through the use of a wide range of hops, malts and the innovation and passion of the brewing team. Four years later, the brewery had picked up scores of national and international awards and had outgrown its 10-barrel brewery. So in September 2009 the operation moved to a new state-of-the-art brewery, complete with bottling line, so that the brewers could increase their range of beers. Jaipur is a citrus dominated IPA, which starts out softly, has a strong hoppy honeyed centre, and a long, bitter finish.

Jambe-de-Bois

PRODUCER: Brasserie de la Senne

AREA OF ORIGIN: Brussels, Belgium

VARIETY: Tripel

ABV: 8.0%

WEBSITE: www.brasseriedelasenne.be

The beers of Brasserie de la Senne are produced by two passionate brewers from Brussels – Yvan De Baets and Bernard Leboucq – who started making beer together in 2006. They moved to their present site in 2010. They work in a small brewery that honours the traditional ways of brewing beer: unfiltered, unpasteurised, free of any additives, and using only the finest raw materials of the highest quality. Their stock in trade is fine ales, but they have created blends using lambic beer in the past. Jambe-de-Bois is a tripel beer but it stands apart from other beers in its category because it has a distinctive, sour, hoppy flavour.

Jambo!

PRODUCER: The Wild Beer Co

AREA OF ORIGIN: Evercreech, England

VARIETY: Flavoured stout

ABV: 8.5%

WEBSITE: www.wildbeerco.com

Everything about the Wild Beer Co is appealing, from the fantastic beer recipes and great beer names, to the smart and stylish packaging. Most craft brewers demonstrate their love for what they do, but here pride just flows through the many and varied products. The brewery is crowdfunded and welcomed 2000 new investors in 2016, with plans to build a new brewery in the very near future.

Jambo is a rich and strong imperial stout brewed with raspberries and Valrhona cocoa nibs. It has a delicious tartness and bitter chocolate. It comes in big 750ml bottles to encourage sharing. Perfect for winter nights.

THE **WILD BEER** CO

JAMBO!

Imperial stout + Chocolate
+ Raspberries

DRINK WILDLY DIFFERENT

Kaleidoscope

PRODUCER: Wiper and True

AREA OF ORIGIN: Bristol, England

VARIETY: Pale ale

ABV: 4.2%

WEBSITE: www.wiperandtrue.com

Wiper and True make great beers, epitomising what craft brewing is all about. The people behind this brewery started learning about brewing on a kitchen stove with pots, pans and a hotchpotch of raw ingredients. They took every opportunity to visit breweries and to learn from other brewers before launching their business. They're keen on experimentation, adding wild ingredients such as chillies and blackberries, and ageing beer in different woods.

Kaleidoscope is a true beauty of a beer, and as fresh and sharp as a pale ale can be. It is soft, fruity and floral with a light, hoppy taste with touches of citrus, tropical, and peachy notes. The flavour is sweet, with some pleasant bitterness in the finish.

Kasteel Rouge

PRODUCER: Bierkasteel Van Honsebrouck

AREA OF ORIGIN: Belgium

VARIETY: Red ale

ABV: 8.0%

WEBSITE: www.vanhonsebrouck.be

One of the most exciting things about the modern craft brewing scene is the way that brewers are prepared to break out of formulaic beer styles and attempt to produce something new, exciting and different. Kasteel Rouge is a stunning example of this trend. It is a delicious, rich cherry beer that blends Kasteel's quadruple-style beer Donker with a cherry liqueur. Donker is a spicy beer with rich, deep chocolate notes. The cherries provide a rich fruitiness to the beer. It is one of the tastiest beers you'll ever find, with a punchy alcoholic bite and intensely complex flavour.

Keller Pils

PRODUCER: Lost and Grounded Brewery

AREA OF ORIGIN: Bristol, England

VARIETY: Hop bitter lager

ABV: 4.8%

WEBSITE: www.lostandgrounded.co.uk

Lost and Grounded is a serious and sizeable brewing operation in Bristol, South West England, which takes its influences from Germany. Its brewhouse comes from Freising in Germany, and includes a traditional lactic acid propagation plant. This means that the brewery produces a sour wort in the same way as German brewers, giving the brewery the flexibility to make European styles of beer.

Keller Pils combines German pilsner malt with three traditional hops for a simple, refreshing and clean hop bitter lager. The resulting lager has light grassy undertones, but the main flavour is malty, with some citrus notes, particularly orange and lemon.

Kernel Pale Ale

PRODUCER: The Kernel Brewery

AREA OF ORIGIN: London, England

VARIETY: Pale ale

ABV: 5.3%

WEBSITE: www.thekernelbrewery.com

There have been some dark mumblings about the future of craft beer as signs in America suggest the popularity of it may be peaking. That's certainly not the case elsewhere. Take Kernel. It has become so popular it has had to close its over-busy bar and focus just on bottle sales. Some of its best beers are pale ales, and it sells a range of them made with a range of hops, and will add twists, such as oats for creaminess, when it feels inclined. Kernel is highly regarded and has been described as 'craft brewing royalty'.

Kingpin

PRODUCER: Brewdog

AREA OF ORIGIN: Ellon, Scotland

VARIETY: Lager

ABV: 4.7%

WEBSITE: www.brewdog.com

When you read the Brewdog story it's all made to sound so easy – and, to some degree, it was. Take two very gifted beer makers of fearless disposition with an instinct for publicity, and throw in an irreverent, anti-establishment attitude, and you've got the makings of a good business. But whether they admit it or not, James Watt and Martin Dickie have excellent business acumen too, and they have barely put a foot wrong. It helps when you have beer such as this. Brewed with 100% malt and a big wave of hops, this cold-conditioned lager is at the forefront of giving lager a good name. Early on there's a wave of robust, full-bodied malt character, then spicy citrus notes coat the mouth. The palate also has some green fruit notes. An assertive bitter finish brings everything to a more-ish and balanced conclusion.

Kiwanda

PRODUCER: Pelican Pub & Brewing

AREA OF ORIGIN: Pacific City, USA

VARIETY: Cream ale

ABV: 5.4%

WEBSITE: www.pelicanbrewing.com

Pelican Pub & Brewing started life at a stunning site on the edge of the Oregon coastline, more than two decades ago, and today has sites along the coast. The offering is a simple but effective one – good beer, good food, and good company, without gimmicks. Kiwanda Cream Ale celebrates Cape Kiwanda, the starting point of the stunning Three Capes Scenic Route and the birthplace of Pelican Brewing Company. Inspired by one of America's traditional 19th-century beer styles, Kiwanda has a floral aroma, refreshing body and a clean, snappy finish.

Kiwi Rising

PRODUCER: Jack's Abby

AREA OF ORIGIN: Framingham, USA

VARIETY: lager

ABV: 8.5%

WEBSITE: www.jacksabby.com

Jack's Abby was founded in 2011 by three brothers, Jack, Eric, and Sam Hendler, and has expanded rapidly, becoming an important part of the craft brewing scene in the American Northeast. Since opening, the brewery has tripled in size and is continuing to grow. Jack's Abby now has a bar and kitchen and serves up fresh wood-fired pizza alongside great beer. The brewery makes craft lager, and Kiwi Rising is an intensely hoppy and strong lager that is described as a Double IPA. Over four pounds of New Zealand hops (Kiwi Hops) are used in progressively larger hop additions throughout the brewing process. The high strength and big flavours make for an unforgettable beer.

INTENSELY HOPPY

JACK'S ABBY
CRAFT LAGERS

KIWI
RISING

DOUBLE IPL

Kuehnes Blonde

PRODUCER: Koehn Kunz Rosen

AREA OF ORIGIN: Mainz, Germany

VARIETY: Wheat beer

ABV: 4.9%

WEBSITE: www.kuehnkunzrosen.de

This is a wheat beer, also known as a wit beer, and it bears all the hallmarks of classic wheat beers – it's cloudy, unfiltered and spicy, due to a mix of herbs and spices that may include coriander and orange peel. The style has become very popular in the United States but beware, there are a lot of badly made wheat beers that are sickly sweet and cloying. This one isn't a bit like that at all. It's a beauty. At the time of writing there was no Koehn Kunz Rosen brewery and the brewers describe making their beers 'as gypsy brewers at the Brauhaus Binkert in Breitenguessbach near Bamberg'.

La Corne du Bois des Pendus Tripel

PRODUCER: Six North

AREA OF ORIGIN: Scotland

VARIETY: Tripel

ABV: 10.0%

WEBSITE: www.lacorneduboisdespendus.be/
la-corne-triple

The folk behind Six North call themselves the Belgian
Brewers of Scotland, and there is no comparable
operation to it. Based in the North East of Scotland,
which is six degrees North of Belgium, the brewery
services a range of its own beer bars in cities such as
Aberdeen, Glasgow and Edinburgh. Each venue has a
tasting room, waiter service, and regular tastings and
sessions. The beers emulate a range of
Belgian beer styles. La Corne du Bois des
Pendus Tripel is a highly aromatic and
floral beer that is very drinkable, despite
its high strength. The brewery says it is
not as bitter as its mild blonde sister,
La Corne du Bois des Pendus Blonde.
It is served in a horn-shaped glass.

Lazy Haze

PRODUCER: Tatton Brewery

AREA OF ORIGIN: Knutsford, Cheshire

VARIETY: Summer ale

ABV: 3.7%

WEBSITE: www.tattonbrewery.co.uk

The Tatton Brewery in England's North West is a delightful combination of traditional and well made beers made in a modern environment. The brewery was set up by Gregg Sawyer, and he and his team put a great deal of emphasis on making exceptional beer. To do so, Tatton uses a yeast that was last used by Chesters Brewery more than 50 years ago. The brewery produces four regular beers and compliments them with seasonal and occasional beers.

Lazy Haze is fabulous. It is described as a summer ale and is brewed with a tea infusion. It's very pleasant, and very drinkable. It's a light, soft, sweet and rounded ale with honey, light citrus and strawberry notes. The tea infusion gives the beer a herbal under base, and the relatively low alcohol content make the whole experience very sessionable. Tastes great in winter, and no doubt is wonderful when the sun is beating down.

Mariana Trench

PRODUCER: Weird Beard Brew Co.

AREA OF ORIGIN: London, England

VARIETY: Pale ale

ABV: 5.3%

WEBSITE: www.weirdbeardbrewco.com

As the name might suggest, the folk behind Weird Beard have attitude. They are proud to be non-conformist, say they refuse to be stereotyped, and make big, bold in-your-face beers with flair and creativity.

Their core beers include Black Perle, Little Things That Kill, and this one, Mariana Trench, which is named after a huge scar-shaped ditch at the bottom of the deepest oceans midway between Japan and Papua New Guinea. It's named as such because the beer is a Transatlantic pale ale, made with New Zealand Pacific Gem and American Citra hops. It has a flavour that includes orange and lemon, mango and lychee.

Midnight Sun

PRODUCER: Williams Bros. Brewing Co.

AREA OF ORIGIN: Alloa, Scotland

VARIETY: Porter

ABV: 5.6%

WEBSITE: www.williamsbrosbrew.com

Williams Bros. describes itself as a 'brotherhood of brewers' and is located in Alloa, Scotland. The brewery is based in the building that used to house George Younger's bottling plant, in a town that was once described as Scotland's brewing capital. The Williams brothers, Bruce and Scott, originally worked in the family business, a home-brew shop in Glasgow. But when a woman came in with an ancient beer recipe she wanted to make for her family, she agreed to allow Bruce to use it. And from there the brewing business grew. Midnight Sun has been described as an instant classic. Made with chocolate malt and oats, with a spicy bite of root ginger.

Mont des Cats Bière Trappiste

PRODUCER: Abbaye Sainte Marie du Mont des Cats

AREA OF ORIGIN: Godewaersvelde, France

VARIETY: Belgian-style pale ale

ABV: 7.6%

WEBSITE: www.trappistbeer.net/othertrappistbreweries/
mont_des_cats_page1EN.htm

Abbaye Sainte Marie du Mont des Cats is a monastery in Northern France, a few miles from the Belgian border and, like most monasteries, it is economically self-sufficient due to its dairy products, such as its exceptional cheeses. The monastery had a brewery, too, but brewing ceased in 1905 and the brewery was destroyed towards the end of the First World War and was never rebuilt.

In 2011 the monastery returned to beer production to drive revenue, and asked the famous monastic brewery of Chimay to produce this beer to their own recipe. This is a rich and flavoursome beer packed with fruit flavours, evolving into a hoppy mouth-coating body, and by the long finish a pleasant bitterness develops.

Mr Trotter's Chestnut Ale

PRODUCER: Mr Trotter's

AREA OF ORIGIN: Lancaster, England

VARIETY: Chestnut ale

ABV: 4.0%

WEBSITE: www.mrtrotters.com

Mr Trotter's is a luxury pork scratching producer – if there can be such a thing – created by a team that includes food writers and critics Tom Parker-Bowles and Matthew Fort, and beer supremo Rupert Ponsonby. The idea was to produce high-class scratchings to accompany fine craft beer, and since the company's launch in 2011 there have been a number of spin-off brands, including this ale. Mr Trotter's Chestnut Ale is made with Maris Otter malt, English Cascade and Braming Cross hops, as well as sweet, roasted chestnuts, which are a favourite of pigs, apparently. The roasted chestnuts serve to give the beer a rich, creamy texture and a sweet, honeyed note. This is the only chestnut ale brewed in the United Kingdom.

Noblesse VSOP

PRODUCER: De Dochter van de Korenaar

AREA OF ORIGIN: Baarle Hertog Belgium

VARIETY: Kölsch-style blonde beer

ABV: 5.5%

WEBSITE: www.dedochtervandekorenaar.be

The name of this brewery means 'ear of the corn' and it is an ancient term for beer, taken from a quote from Emperor Charles (1500–88): 'I prefer the juice of the ear of the corn, better than the blood of grapes.'

The brewery is modern and was set up in 2007 by Dutch couple Monique and Roland Mengerink to bring brewing back to Baarle Hertog. It is a small and traditional brewery specialising in a range of classic beer styles. So small, in fact, that it is sited in the back garden of the family home. Noblesse is an easy to drink and accessible blonde beer, with a relatively moderate alcoholic strength. It is designed to be the bridge from lager to more testing Belgian beer styles.

Old Freddy Walker

PRODUCER: Moor Beer Company

AREA OF ORIGIN: Bristol, England

VARIETY: Old ale

ABV: 7.5%

WEBSITE: www.moorbeer.co.uk

Moor Beer Company is named after the Levels and Moors region of Somerset in the South West of England. The brewery was originally located there but this version of it is based in the heart of the city of Bristol, near the railway station. It is owned by Californian Justin Hawke, who bought the defunct business in 2007 and set about making quality beer. The current site became the brewery's home in 2014 and boasts a shop and brewery tap. Old Freddy Walker is the brewery's strongest beer and it's a rich, fruity and flavoursome old ale that tastes great by the fire in winter but can be enjoyed all year round. If you see it at a beer festival, grab it – it tends to be one of the fastest sellers.

MOOR
BEER COMPANY

OLD FREDDY WALKER

This rich, dark, full-bodied old ale is like liquid Christmas pudding, sure to bring you festive joy. One for the connoisseur.

7.5%

BOTTLE CONDITIONED BEER

BREWED & BOTTLED IN SOMERSET UK

Passion Drop

PRODUCER: Fourpure Brewing Co.

AREA OF ORIGIN: London, England

VARIETY: IPA

ABV: 4.7%

WEBSITE: www.fourpure.com

The company's name Fourpure refers to the fact that this family-run brewery puts an emphasis on the four key ingredients of its beers – grain, yeast, hops and water. This is no small-time operation – the main brewery is a sizeable one, producing all-year-round and keg beers, but it also offers a number of one-off beers, available in the brewery tap room and in crowler (large can) format. It also has an in-house barrel ageing programme, which is focused on sours and darker ales. This is made by overloading the fermenter with passionfruit, to produce beer with tropical fruit notes and a subtle, refreshing tartness.

Peanut Butter Milk Stout

PRODUCER: Tailgate Brewery

AREA OF ORIGIN: Nashville, USA

VARIETY: Milk stout

ABV: 5.8%

WEBSITE: www.tailgatebeer.com

Only in America … and they're not the only brewers
doing weird things like this, either. Tailgate is a brewery
in Nashville, Tennessee, and it specialises in small batch
craft beers, many of them based on Belgian styles.
While they're pretty serious about their beers, they're big
about experimenting with flavours, too. Their creations
include Pineapple Tart Saison, Apple Spice Sour,
Cinnamon Toast Brunch, and These Strawberries Taste
Like Strawberries Sour (yum).

Peanut Butter Milk Stout is an all-year-round release
that won World's Best Experimental Flavoured Beer at
the 2015 World Beer Awards. It does what it says on
the tin – with roasted peanut notes and a big, creamy
chocolate and coffee hit on the palate.

Peppercorn Saison

PRODUCER: 3 Stars Brewing Co.

AREA OF ORIGIN: Washington DC, USA

VARIETY: Farmhouse ale

ABV: 6.5%

WEBSITE: 3starsbrewing.com

3 Stars Brewing Co. was set up by long-term friends Dave Coleman and Mike McGarvey, whose aim was to build a brewery to produce quality craft beer. They started home brewing in Mike's basement, experimenting with recipes. Then, when the time was right, they started searching for funds and a premises in Washington. The brewery started up in 2012 and the duo have produced about 50 different beers since.

Peppercorn Saison is a Belgian-style farmhouse ale and is made all year round. Grains in its production include wheat, and the hops are Centennial and Cascade. This results in a beer that is described as having a sweet and slightly fruity nose, with hints of grass and coriander on the palate, and a clean dry finish, with some citrus.

Polygraph

PRODUCER: Salopian Brewery

AREA OF ORIGIN: Shrewsbury, England

VARIETY: Stout

ABV: 7.4%

WEBSITE: www.salopianbrewery.co.uk

Salopian means 'of Shrewsbury' and this brewery is based in the West England market town. It is older than most craft breweries, having been set up in 1994 by Martin Barry at his pub in West Wales. He moved to Shrewsbury in 1995.

Salopian grew organically, carrying out contract brewing at the outset and starting to brew its own beers when progressive beer taxes were changed in 2002. Since then it has changed the style of beer it makes and has expanded from a tiny two-barrel plant to the 50-barrel plant it has now.

Polygraph is a full-bodied stout that has dark chocolate, espresso coffee, liquorice and tart, dark fruits in the mix.

Proper Job

PRODUCER: St Austell Brewery

AREA OF ORIGIN: St Austell, Cornwall

VARIETY: IPA

ABV: 5.5%

WEBSITE: www.staustellbrewery.co.uk

St Austell Brewery is in Cornwall, in the far South West of England, and it is one of Britain's most respected breweries, with a history stretching back to 1851, when it was founded by Walter Hicks. The brewery has operated ever since, remains completely independent, and is still a family-owned business. It has an impressively diverse business with wine, hotels, pubs, inns and, of course, beer.

Proper Job is one of the brewery's core range beers, served on draught but also bottled. It's an IPA made with just Maris Otter barley, and it's bottle conditioned, which means that yeast in the bottle ensures fermentation continues after bottling. Very hoppy and intense.

BOTTLE CONDITIONED

PROPER
JOB

POWERFULLY
HOPPED

INDIA PALE ALE

ALC. 5.5 % VOL

Punk IPA

PRODUCER: Brewdog

AREA OF ORIGIN: Ellon, Scotland

VARIETY: IPA

ABV: 5.6%

WEBSITE: www.brewdog.com

Few brewing stories have managed to achieve the success of Brewdog. In 2007 two Scottish friends decided to brew their own beer. They borrowed money, started making the sort of craft beer they would want to drink, hand-filled bottles and sold them at local markets. Today the company has a second brewery in America, has opened bars in high streets across Britain, has 750 employees and a staggering 55000 shareholders. Brewdog's flagship beer is Punk IPA, and its creators say it 'charges the barricades to fly its colours from the ramparts – full-on, full flavour; at full throttle.' It's a beer that has been the antithesis of bland beer. The layers of new world hops create an explosion of tropical fruit and an all-out riot of grapefruit, pineapple and lychee before a spiky bitter finish.

Quartz Heart

PRODUCER: Quartz Brewing

AREA OF ORIGIN: Kings Bromley, England

VARIETY: Premium bitter

ABV: 4.6%

WEBSITE: www.quartzbrewing.co.uk

Quartz Brewing's moniker is 'redefining the art of craft brewing' and it has a small but stylish selection of beers. The brewery was originally set up by Scott Barnett in 2005, but the team behind it now represent more than 50 years experience in the industry, and they claim to be one of the most technologically advanced microbreweries in the United Kingdom. Most of the brewery's output goes to pubs and clubs as draught beer, but Quartz has a beautifully packaged set of bottle beers. Heart is part of the brewery's core range and it has a fruit and vanilla nose, with fruitiness extended into the taste, some camp coffee, fresh maltiness and nuttiness. It also has a pleasant and lengthy finish.

Quintet

PRODUCER: Wiper and True

AREA OF ORIGIN: Bristol, England

VARIETY: IPA

ABV: 6.2%

WEBSITE: www.wiperandtrue.com

Wiper and True's beers are often difficult to pigeonhole. Its Peel and Stone, for instance, is an India Pale Ale but it takes on tones of a Belgian beer through the use of Morello cherries and orange zest. It has soft fruit aromas with orange citrus and cherry jam notes.

Some beers are works in progress that evolve over time, and Quintet is one of these. The strength of this beer varies from 6.0% to 7.0%, and the taste changes as a result. That's because five different types of hops are used in each batch, but the hops change. The key to each batch, though, is its taste. The idea is to make as full-bodied an IPA as possible. Expect a lively, refreshing and pleasantly sharp taste sensation.

Radical Road

PRODUCER: Stewart Brewing

AREA OF ORIGIN: Edinburgh, Scotland

VARIETY: IPA

ABV: 6.4%

WEBSITE: www.stewartbrewing.co.uk

Breweries can be pretty dull places, often no more than a collection of stainless steel ugly-looking machines in a damp warehouse. But Stewart Brewing has custom-built premises, which it says is very much focused on the public. The Stewarts say they are proud to show off what they do, and they have lots of incredible facilities on site for guests to explore.

Radical Road is from the brewery's hop series and is triple hopped using three American hops – Cascade, Magnum and Centennial.

This beer is bursting with flavour, with sweet and sour bouncing off each other and grapefruit happiness rubbing up against malty bitterness. It packs a punch yet is still very more-ish.

Red Sky

PRODUCER: Shenanigans Brewing Company

AREA OF ORIGIN: Australia

VARIETY: American-style IPA

ABV: 6.5%

WEBSITE: www.shenanigansbrewing.com

Shenanigans Brewing Company was set up in Australia by friends Sam Haldane and Dan Beers. Their aim is to make experimental and innovative beers by infusing a range of ingredients into their recipes. Guava, pineapple, jalapeños and coffee have all featured in recipes. The duo don't have a brewery so they 'gypsy brew' in a number of breweries in the Sydney area.

Red Sky is an American-style IPA infused with jasmine and hibiscus flowers. The floral notes on the nose and palate come from the jasmine, while the hibiscus gives the beer a slightly tart and refreshing note. American and Australian hops provide the citrus and passionfruit notes.

Rhetoric Edition 4.1

PRODUCER: Hardknott Brewery

AREA OF ORIGIN: Cumbria, England

VARIETY: Imperial stout

ABV: 11.0%

WEBSITE: www.hardknott.com

Hardknott is very clear about what it is trying to achieve; it wants to make the best beers to come from the great Western Lakes of North West England. The brewery was established in 2005 and moved into much bigger premises as it won people over to its beers, many of them influenced by the great American and Belgian beers. Rhetoric Edition 4.1 is its progressive and experimental range. Each release is an attempt to take beer in new directions. Rhetoric Edition 4.1 is a large stout made with peat-smoked malt. The result is genuinely different, with smoke, chocolate, coffee and liquorice all found in this fantastic beer.

Rübaeus

PRODUCER: Founders Brewing Co.

AREA OF ORIGIN: Grand Rapids, USA

VARIETY: Fruit beer

ABV: 5.7%

WEBSITE: www.foundersbrewing.com

Everyone and their dog is now bravely brewing big tasting gonzo craft beers, but turn the clock back to the late 1990s and that wasn't the case at all. So when Mike Stevens and Dave Engbers decided to launch their own brewery, the response of friends and family was 'mixed'. And they nearly blew it by playing it safe and bland. Then they took a huge gamble, turned to powerful, flavoursome in-your-face beers ... and they haven't looked back since. Rübaeus is a fine example of what they're about – a fresh raspberry punch with refreshing sweet and tart notes in perfect balance.

Saison à la Provision

PRODUCER: Burning Sky

AREA OF ORIGIN: Firle, England

VARIETY: Saison beer

ABV: 6.5%

WEBSITE: www.burningskybeer.com

Burning Sky was created with the intention of producing punchy hop-dominant pale ales and Belgian-style beers. It is located in farm buildings close to a quirky village in the picturesque South Downs. The first beer was produced in Autumn 2013 and immediately started picking up awards. Since then the brewery has installed oak foudres for ageing beers and a traditional coolship vessel, used to produce spontaneously fermented beers with natural yeasts. Saison à la Provision beer is first fermented with saison yeast, then undergoes a secondary fermentation with a blend of cask bacteria. The result is a tart, crisp, slightly sour and refreshing saison beer.

Salty Kiss Gooseberry Gose

PRODUCER: Magic Rock Brewing

AREA OF ORIGIN: Huddersfield, England

VARIETY: Gose

ABV: 4.1%

WEBSITE: www.magicrockbrewing.com

Magic Rock Brewing is a collaboration between brothers Richard and Jonny Burhouse and head brewer Stuart Ross, and they started making beer in 2011. In its first year Magic Rock was named Second Best New Brewery in the World by respected independent online site Rate Beer. The brewery expanded twice in 2012 and moved entirely in 2015, doubling its capacity. The brewery now employs 30 people.

Salty Kiss Gooseberry Gose is the brewery's version of a German Gose, flavoured with fruit, sea buckthorn and sea salt. Gose is an ancient wheated style of beer made in Northern Germany but which had become extinct. It's been revived by craft brewers and this version is as savoury as you might expect – with salty and sour notes, and polite fruit notes.

Shape Shifter

PRODUCER: Fourpure Brewing Co.

AREA OF ORIGIN: London, England

VARIETY: IPA

ABV: 5.9%

WEBSITE: www.fourpure.com

Fourpure was set up by brothers Dan and Tom Lowe in 2013 in London, and it's a sizeable business, with 24 fermentation tanks, of mainly 75 hl capacity, but with some smaller ones for innovative and exciting new creations. In addition to the brewery itself, there are three other warehouses dedicated to packaging and distribution. The growing team were awarded the 2017 Most Innovative and Brewery Business titles by the Society of Independent Brewers.

Shape Shifter is a fruity IPA with Citra, Centennial and Mosaic hops to give it a grapefuit, pineapple and mango tang, delivered by a weighty 5.9% ABV. This has a particularly nice long bitter finish. Classy.

Siberia Rhubarb Saison

PRODUCER: Ilkley Brewery

AREA OF ORIGIN: Ilkley, England

VARIETY: Saison beer

ABV: 5.9%

WEBSITE: www.ilkleybrewery.co.uk

Ilkley is in Yorkshire, Northern England. It's a place where you can walk on the moor without your hat. And a flavoured saison beer coming from a brewery there seems a little incongruous – even if it is made with rhubarb. Siberia was created for the first time in 2012, when the brewery invited beer expert Melissa Cole to help them produce a saison beer with a Yorkshire twist. This is clever stuff. The rhubarb was stewed with vanilla to provide balance, and then the fruit's natural sourness was used to balance the earthiness of Saison yeast.

'This beer is tart in all the right places,' says the brewery, and it is, by gum.

Single Hop Kohatu Mango Femme Fatale

PRODUCER: Evil Twin Brewing

AREA OF ORIGIN: Denmark

VARIETY: IPA with mango

ABV: 5.5%

WEBSITE: www.eviltwin.dk

Evil Twin Brewing is something of an enigma. It is the creation of Jeppe Jarnit-Bjergso, a Dane with a Danish email address, though the head office of the company is in America. It seems that the company works with 10 specially selected craft breweries and seeks out unusual and flavoursome brews. This one, then, was brewed by Westbrook Brewing Company.

This beer comes at you from two directions. On the one hand, there's the attractive mango fruits, and on the other you have Kohatu's piney, alluring tastes. Take those on board and you have a desirable fruity, tropical, crisp, tart beer.

Sour Grapes

PRODUCER: Lovibonds Brewery

AREA OF ORIGIN: Henley-on-Thames, England

VARIETY: Sour beer

ABV: 5.4%

WEBSITE: www.lovibonds.com

Lovibonds is the brewery home of American brewer Jeff Rosenmeier, who moved to Henley-On-Thames and fell in love with it. Sour Grapes is the result of serendipity. It was meant to be a batch of Henley Gold but it seems that *Lactobacillus* bacteria had outcompeted the beer yeast, which had grown weak. It was sour – and wonderful. But Jeff wasn't finished yet. He put his brew into red wine casks made up of 75% Sour Grapes and 25% Henley Gold, along with three starter cultures from the dregs of previous favourite beers. Three years later and a mix of two barrels make the beer on sale now. The brewery now describes the beer as sour and funky. How's that for thinking out of the box?

Sourdough

PRODUCER: The Wild Beer Co

AREA OF ORIGIN: Shepton Mallet, England

VARIETY: Sour beer

ABV: 3.6%

WEBSITE: www.wildbeerco.com

Sourdough has been familiar to bakers, brewers and distillers for thousands of years, and they are drawn together because of the role of yeasts and natural bacteria that make for distinctive flavours in all three processes. This beer, then, is a combination of baking and brewing. This is a combination of the old and the new, and even before it had a brewery the Wild Beer Co was talking to Hobbs House Bakery's Tom Herbert about making a beer with his 58-year-old sourdough yeast. It took a lot of trialling but this is the result. It is a blend of beers from 24 ex-wine casks and two bourbon casks. This is a very gentle, tangy and fruity beer.

SOURDOUGH

Sourdough Culture
+ Oak Barrel Fermentation

HOBBS HOUSE BAKERY & THE WILD BEER CO.

Stateside Saison

PRODUCER: Stillwater Artisanal

AREA OF ORIGIN: Baltimore, USA

VARIETY: Saison farmhouse ale

ABV: 6.8%

WEBSITE: www.stillwater-artisanal.com

The website for Stillwater Artisanal is very modern, which is a clue to Brian Strumke, the person behind this operation. Strumke was once an internationally renowned electronica DJ. Really. He started experimenting with weird and wonderful beer concoctions and eventually signed a deal with a distribution company to take his beers around the world. Brian was used to travelling the world and using different studios for recording, so it made sense to him to be one of the first 'gypsy brewers'. He has created 50 Stillwater creations in 12 different countries. Stateside Saison uses European malts and fresh aromatic hops from New Zealand and America fermented with a classic farmhouse ale yeast. It is, says Strumke, a combination of old world tradition with new world innovation.

Sun Dazed

PRODUCER: Old Town Brewing Company

AREA OF ORIGIN: Portland, USA

VARIETY: Kölsch-style ale

ABV: 4.8%

WEBSITE: www.otbrewing.com

Old Town Brewing Company is based at the heart of one of America's best drinks cities and has its operation divided between a tap room downtown and the brewery itself. It's proud of its Portland leagues.

'Old Town was founded by the idea that the best beer is born of your surroundings,' says the brewery. 'You may consider this our love letter to the Pacific Northwest.'

The brewery makes a wide range of beers and sells them alongside their award-winning pizzas. Sun Dazed is Kölsch-style ale, which comes from Köln in Germany. It is a top-fermented beer made mainly with Pilsner malt.

Old Town describes Sun Dazed as being 'like backyard barbecues, lazy river floats, second degree sunburns, and a hint of summer flings.' That works.

Sunday

PRODUCER: And Union

AREA OF ORIGIN: Bavaria, Germany

VARIETY: Pale ale

ABV: 5.5%

WEBSITE: www.andunion.com

And Union was founded in 2007 by a father and son and a long-time business partner, who happened to be a friend. They work with four small Bavarian breweries that are family-owned and family-run. The company is proud to be small and traditional, but with a modern approach to brewing. The breweries they work with produce between 10 000 hl and 180 000 hl per annum. The company has an extensive range of beers and this one is a light and refreshing easy drinking pale ale. Tastes great with seafood and mature cheeses. Here there is orange peel and fresh flowers on the nose, tangerine and grapefruit on the palate, with rich malt. The finish has citrus and intense hoppiness.

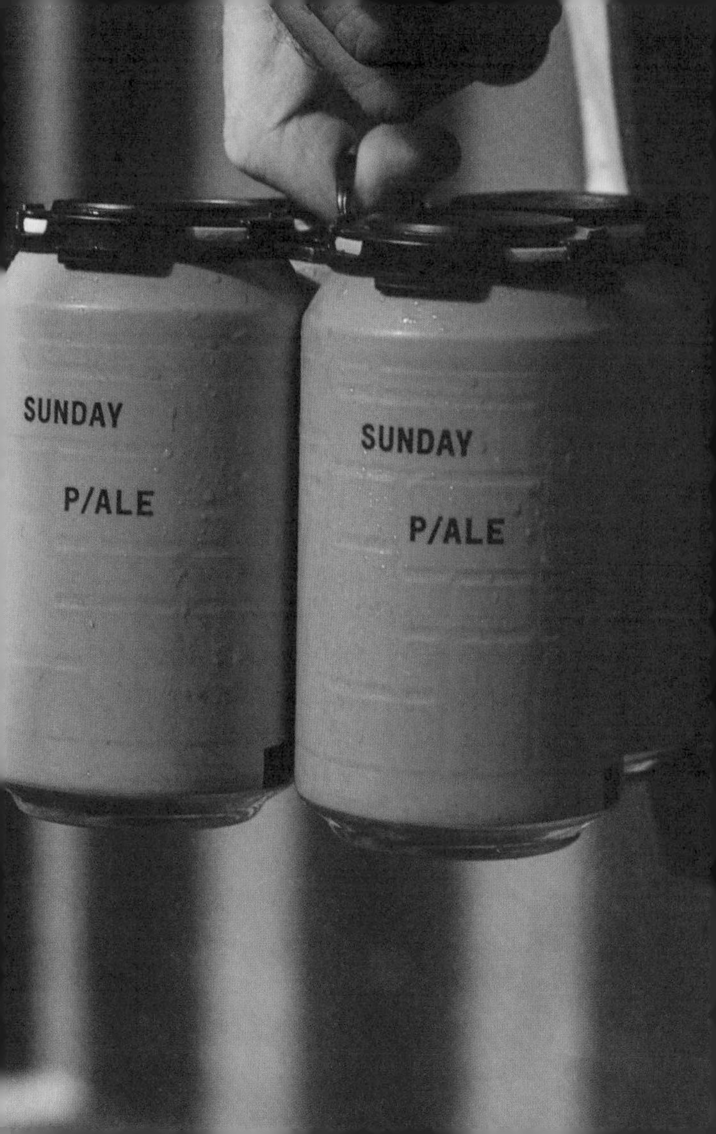
SUNDAY
P/ALE
SUNDAY
P/ALE

Tempest Harvest

PRODUCER: Tempest Brew Co.

AREA OF ORIGIN: Kelso, Scotland

VARIETY: IPA

ABV: 6.7%

WEBSITE: www.tempestbrewco.com

Tempest is a brewing partnership between a Scottish man and a New Zealand woman, who met in Canada, have lived in New Zealand, have travelled the world, and are now creating fascinating beers in the Borders of Scotland. They are doing so on the back of a gastro pub called The Cobbles, which they resurrected, decorated, and turned into a quality outlet. Tempest Brewing Co. opened in 2010 in an old dairy. Tempest Harvest is a Belgian IPA hybrid, with a Belgian strain of yeast, and each edition varies. There are distinct orange notes in this version, and fruity spiciness.

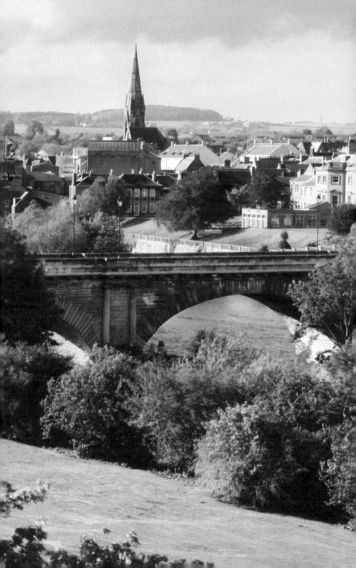

Three Grain Belgian Blonde

PRODUCER: Brew By Numbers

AREA OF ORIGIN: London, England

VARIETY: Blonde beer

ABV: 6.9%

WEBSITE: www.brewbynumbers.com

Brew By Numbers is a London-based microbrewery formed by two friends who met in China while rock climbing. They both came to the idea of brewing independently but when they met up again in London in 2011 they decided to work together on a brewery project. Since then they have learned rapidly and now they make scores of seasonal and core beers, using modern marketing and techniques to add a twist to some of the world's greatest beer styles. Three grain is made in small batches but is typically 6.9% ABV and is aged in new oak barrels. The grains are un-malted wheat, oats and barley. This has effervescent and yeasty notes with strong fruit and spice notes, particularly lemon dry hop. The taste is fruity, with banana, apricot, pear, and raisin. The taste is sweet with hop dryness in the finish. More spice in the finish.

Ticketybrew Dubbel

PRODUCER: Ticketybrew

AREA OF ORIGIN: Stalybridge, England

VARIETY: Dubbel

ABV: 6.5%

WEBSITE: www.ticketybrew.co.uk

Ticketybrew is all about yeast. It particularly loves Belgian yeasts and uses them in many of its beers, including this core beer. In 2016 the brewery started experimenting with other yeasts, and in 2017 it went a stage further, mixing yeasts to create new strains, or reinforcing individual flavour profiles.

Dubbel is based on the renowned Belgian beer style. It is a dark beer but it contains no roasted malts, giving it a smooth taste. The deep burnt red colour is achieved by adding a dark sugar syrup. Ticketybrew uses the light and classic German Nobel hop to create a light spiciness and a mellow bitterness. Expect raisins, chocolate, cinnamon, and baked apples in the mix.

Tournay Noire

PRODUCER: Brasserie de Cazeau

AREA OF ORIGIN: Templeuve, Belgium

VARIETY: Stout

ABV: 7.6%

WEBSITE: www.brasseriedecazeau.be

Brasserie de Cazeau is a family craft brewery with a history stretching back to 1753. It has had eight generations of enthusiastic brewers since then, but it is quick to point out that while tradition remains very important to it, that doesn't mean it won't innovate and experiment in search of new tastes. So while its beers are neither filtered nor pasteurised, and are re-fermented in the bottle, new types of hops and potential beer styles are being tested. Currently five beers are produced at the brewery including this one, which the brewery describes as the best stout in the world and, although it's all a matter of opinion, it's not far wrong. Excellent beer.

Twilight of the Idols

PRODUCER: Hill Farmstead Brewery

AREA OF ORIGIN: Greensboro, USA

VARIETY: Porter

ABV: 7.2%

WEBSITE: www.hillfarmstead.com

It's not every day you come across a beer named after the philosopher Fredrich Nietzsche, but then there's nothing very conventional about this American brewery. It pays homage to the past, and the brewery logo has been retrieved from a sign that hung in the tavern that belonged to the great, great, great grandfather of Shaun Hill, who founded the brewery in 2010.

Hill Farmstead makes scores of beers under collective headings such as 'philisophical series', 'ancestral series' and 'single hop series'.

Twilight of the Idols is a winter porter that is brewed every Autumn with a small amount of coffee as well as cinnamon, and aged on vanilla pods. Those three influences come through clearly on the palate.

TWILIGHT OF THE IDOLS
(GÖTZEN-DÄMMERUNG)

PORTER BREWED WITH COFFEE
AND AGED ON VANILLA BEANS

Urban Fox

PRODUCER: Bootleg Brewing Co.

AREA OF ORIGIN: Chorlton, England

VARIETY: Red IPA

ABV: 4.4%

WEBSITE: www.bootlegbrewingco.com

Bootleg Brewing Company started brewing in 2010, housed in the Horse & Jockey pub, which is in the shell of a tower that was part of an original disused brewery. Bootleg clearly got it right from the start because two months after opening its first brew picked up its first award. The brewery strongly supports real ale, and not only sponsors several real ale festivals throughout the year, but also holds its own Chorlton Beer Festival. The brewery has now expanded its cask range. Urban Fox is one of its new additions, and is described by Bootleg as 'a cunningly brewed red "rye PA" packed with crisp hops. Crafty, charismatic and doggedly drinkable.' There are lightly toasted grains in the nose. The palate is sweet, with bitter grain husk arriving before toffee and orange peel. The finish is crusty, with some cereal notes. A session beer.

Whitewalker

PRODUCER: North Pier Brewing Company

AREA OF ORIGIN: Benton Harbor, Michigan, USA

VARIETY: White IPA

ABV: 6.4%

WEBSITE: www.northpierbrewing.com

North Pier Brewing Company lies less than a mile from the shores of Lake Michigan. It was founded by husband-and-wife team Jay and Jordan Fettig, out of their love for the craft brewing scene. Having graduated from business school, Jay was confident he could run the business but to ensure top quality beer he turned to brewer Steve Distasio, who had just returned from brewing school in the United Kingdom. The team specialises in Belgian-style beers, and Whitewalker is a mix of wheat for sweet softness, alongside Cashmere and Chinook hops to bring out flavours of pineapple, pine and lemon peel. Belgian yeast is used to further develop the fruity flavours.

Wolf

PRODUCER: Allendale Brewery

AREA OF ORIGIN: Hexham, England

VARIETY: Ruby Ale

ABV: 5.5%

WEBSITE: www.allendalebrewery.com

Originally set up by father and son team Jim and Tom Hick, Allendale has been growing since it was founded in 2006, and Tom now runs the business with his wife Lucy. Head brewer Neil Thomas joined the business in 2009 and brought his exceptional taste palate to the table. Wolf is a core beer for the brewery, available in bottle and on draught, and is a strong ruby ale with a very appealing colour. Wheat and chocolate malts are included in the recipe. A full-bodied beer with a rich fruity taste. Well roasted malts provide caramel on both nose and palate, with toasted buttery croissant. There are notes of raisins and banana in the mix. A touch of blackcurrant on the finish.

Worker's Comp

PRODUCER: Two Roads Brewing Company

AREA OF ORIGIN: Stratford, Connecticut, USA

VARIETY: Farmhouse ale

ABV: 4.8%

WEBSITE: www.tworoadsbrewing.com

Two Roads Brewing Company was set up by four friends who adhere to the concept that life tends to offer two ways to go, and they prefer to choose the road less travelled. In terms of beer making, that means experimenting with unusual brews. To this end they have a series of beers that they group in their 'road less traveled' series.

Worker's Comp is as complex as beers get. It is a traditional farmhouse ale made with a mix of grains including barley, wheat, oats and rye, and a very lively yeast strain to give it verve, fruity notes and spice. This saison beer also has tropical fruit and pepper notes.

Wu Gang Chops The Tree

PRODUCER: Pressure Drop Brewing Company

AREA OF ORIGIN: London, England

VARIETY: Hybrid wheat beer

ABV: 3.8%

WEBSITE: www.pressuredropbrewing.co.uk

Pressure Drop Brewing Company began life as a home operation in the back garden of one of the founders in 2012 and grew from a five-barrel brewery business in 2013 to a 20-barrel one in 2017. It is now based in Tottenham, North London, and the team has opened a tap room.

Wu Gang Chops The Tree is named after a Chinese proverb with a theme too complicated to go into. The brewery made a version of this in 2012. The idea was to combine the flavour of wheat beer – clove, bread and banana – with herbs, to create a beer ideally suited to drink with roast chicken. Don't ask. The team says that it goes with lots of other foods too, including tandoori lamb.

Index

Picture Credits

The publishers would like to thank the following for their assistance with images:

Adnams, Allagash Brewing, Allendale Brewery, Amy Harris / Chorlton Brewing Company, Anchor Brewing Co., And Union Brewery, Battledown Brewey, Bierkasteel Van Honsebrouck, Big Hug Brewing, Bootleg Brewing Co., Boundary Brewery , Bragdy Conwy Brewery, Brasserie de Cazeau, Brewdog, Brooklyn Brewery, Brouwerij De Halve Maan, Brouwerij de Ranke, Brouwerij Hof ten Dormaal, Burning Sky, Buxton Brewery, Camden Town Brewery, Celis Brewery, Cheshire Brewhouse, CREW Republic, Daniel Thwaites, Evil Twin Brewing, Feral Brewing, Figueroa Mountain Brewing Co., Flying Dog, Fourpure Brewing Company, Freedom Brewery, Funky Buddha Brewery / Mitch Wilkinson, Gigantic Brewing Company Gray Box Studios, Gueuzerie Tilquin, Hardknott Brewery, Harvey's Brewery, Harviestoun Brewery, Heavy Seas, Hill Farmstead Brewery, Hopworks Urban Brewery, Howling Hops, Jack's Abby, La Sirène, Lost and Grounded Brewery, Lymestone Brewery, Magic Rock Brewing, Martin House Brewing, Mondo Brewing Company, Mr Trotter's, North Pier Brewing Company, Old Town Brewing Company, Pressure Drop Brewing Company, Quartz Brewing, Salopian Brewery, Shenanigans Brewing Company, Siren Craft Brewing, Six North, Stewart Brewing, Tailgate Brewery, The Durham Brewery, The Lost Abbey, The Ramsgate Brewery, The Wild Beer Co, The Yeastie Boys, Thornbridge Brewery, Two Roads Brewing Company, Victoria Harley, Vocation Brewery, Weird Beard Brew Co., Williams Bros. Brewing Co.

Bernt Rostad (CC by 2.0), Richard Giles (CC BY-SA 2.0), Founders Brewing Co. (CC By 2.0), Christer Edvartsen (CC By 2.0), Stillwater Artisanal (CC By 2.0)

Andris Tkacenko, 5 second Studio, Keith Homan, tusharkoley, Diana Taliun, Sue Leonard Photography / ALL Shutterstock

economic images, PackStock / ALL Alamy Stock Photo

Collins

LITTLE BOOKS

These beautifully presented Little Books make excellent pocket-sized guides, packed with hints and tips.

Bananagrams Secrets
978-0-00-825046-1
£6.99

Bridge Secrets
978-0-00-825047-8
£6.99

101 ways to win at Scrab
978-0-00-758914-2
£6.99

Gin
978-0-00-825810-8
£6.99

Rum
978-0-00-827122-0
£6.99

Whisky
978-0-00-825108-6
£6.99

Scottish Castles
978-0-00-825111-6
£6.99

Scottish Dance
978-0-00-821056-4
£6.99

Scottish History
978-0-00-825110-9
£6.99

Clans and Tartans
978-0-00-825109-3
£6.99

Available to buy from all good booksellers and online.
All titles are also available as ebooks.
www.collins.co.uk

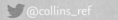 @collins_ref    facebook.com/collinsref